50

THINGS YOU NEED
TO KNOW ABOUT
HEAVEN

50

THINGS YOU NEED
TO KNOW ABOUT
HEAVEN

DR. JOHN HART

BETHANY HOUSE PUBLISHERS
a division of Baker Publishing Group
Minneapolis, Minnesota

© 2014 by Baker Publishing Group

Published by Bethany House Publishers
11400 Hampshire Avenue South
Bloomington, Minnesota 55438
www.bethanyhouse.com

Bethany House Publishers is a division of
Baker Publishing Group, Grand Rapids, Michigan

Printed in the United States of America

Library of Congress Cataloging-in-Publication Data

Hart, John F.
    50 things you need to know about heaven / Dr. John Hart.
        pages cm
    Summary: "College professor Dr. John Hart provides brief, straightforward answers directly from the Bible to fifty of the most commonly asked questions about heaven"— Provided by publisher.
        ISBN 978-0-7642-1166-9 (pbk. : alk. paper)
    1. Heaven—Christianity—Miscellanea. I. Title. II. Title: Fifty things you need to know about heaven.
    BT846.3.H37 2014
    236′.24—dc23   2014003674

14   15   16   17   18   19   20   7   6   5   4   3   2

To my wonderful wife, Cindy.
You are my beautiful partner in life, and I love you.
I owe so much to your wonderful wisdom and support.

To my two sons, J.R. and Chad.
I love you too, and am so proud of you both.

Contents

Introduction

Just scan the Internet. All the polls and surveys taken of Americans over the last ten years or so suggest that more than half of the U.S. population believe in the reality of heaven. This is true of polls taken in Canada and England as well. Heaven is very well-liked. It is universally thought to be a place of great happiness, with freedom from pain and sorrow. So who wouldn't want to believe in heaven?

Our ideas of heaven are drawn from many different sources. Perhaps our ideas are taken from what others have said or from a book we have read. People may have thoughts about heaven influenced by TV and the Internet. The TV show *Touched by an Angel*, which ran from 1994–2003, gave us glimpses of how some thought angels from heaven interact with our lives. But how do we know whether any of these concepts about heaven are true?

This book is designed to be your guide to what the Bible says about heaven. The Bible is a collection of sixty-six books in three different original languages. It was written over a span of two thousand years by forty different authors from three different continents. There are an estimated six trillion Bibles in print today, and the Bible is just as relevant now as it was when the first Bibles were copied on papyrus. Perhaps its wisdom on heaven is worth the investigation. Join with me in the exploration of this fascinating subject.

1 Who goes to heaven?

A story is told of an angel who appeared to a man and granted him any single wish he desired. He thought for a long time, contemplating how he might use this fortunate event to gain a lifetime of wealth. He finally said, "Let me see tomorrow's newspaper." He imagined turning to the stock report and learning what stocks had gained a significant profit overnight. All he had to do was invest his life savings in those stocks and he would make a "killing." The angel obliged, handing him the following day's newspaper. As he turned the pages to find the stock market report, his eyes caught a glance of the obituaries. There was his name!

Few of us plan our days as if we are going to die tomorrow. We frequently joke about it, but we don't take it seriously. Neither do we seriously consider what happens to us after death. We plan our retirement far more conscientiously than we do the "retirement" that follows our retirement. If we think about the afterlife at all, we assure ourselves that we are better than most others and deserve to be in heaven—if it exists.

I once sat on an airplane next to an older man with whom I struck up a conversation. Eventually our discussion led to spiritual things. "On a scale of 1 to 100," I asked, "how sure are you that you are going to heaven?" With a certain confidence, he said, "Oh, 95 percent, I think." It's natural for us to place our confidence in our own goodness and rank ourselves as a viable candidate for heaven.

After all, we think, there are so many other immoral, irreligious, and violent people around us, some even close friends. Compared to such less-than-admirable people, we come out ahead. God must "grade on a curve," and that means I will be in heaven.

In conversations like the one I had with this older man, I rarely find anyone who is 100 percent confident about going to heaven. We would think that a 95 percent assurance—or better, a 99 percent assurance—is well worth the risk. But is it? Would you get on an airplane at Chicago's O'Hare airport—most often ranked the busiest airport in the world—with that kind of risk? If there was a 99 percent chance that your plane would make it to its destination, and only a 1 percent chance it would crash and everyone on board would be killed, would you board that plane? Doesn't that sound like a very good risk?

Statistics show that over 2,400 planes go in and out of O'Hare each day. If 99 percent of those flights arrived or departed safely, and only 1 percent actually crashed, then everyone on board twenty-four flights would die each day! Does that sound like good odds? Not really. So why would you or I ever trust our eternal destiny to 99 percent odds? I know I won't. Jesus said that everyone who believes in him could be completely confident—100 percent confident—that they were bound for heaven. Now *that* is good odds!

There is one condition to get to heaven, and one condition only: to believe in Jesus as the one who can forgive your rebellion against God and take you to heaven when you die. We tend to look at people by their nationality, color of skin, background, talents, or any number of other things. But God looks at the world as two groups: those who believe in Jesus as their only hope for heaven, and those who do not.

It is surprising in our culture how loose we are with the word *believe*. We insist that we should just "believe," giving no real content to what we should believe—just do it. But what good is a faith that has no object or content? It is a faith in the obscure, the indefinite, in nothingness. Others insist that we must just believe in ourselves. But no matter how much I believe in myself, I'm not going to dunk a basketball. I'm five feet six inches, and I can't even touch the net when I jump for it.

The Bible, however, not only warns us against believing in ourselves—it also implies that we need to believe we are sinful, and that we frequently move away from God rather than toward him. The Old Testament prophet Jeremiah said, "The heart is deceitful above all things and beyond cure. Who can understand it?" (Jer. 17:9). Even when we participate in altruistic endeavors, we may deceive ourselves and do so to gain selfish recognition. The prophet Isaiah understood that when he wrote, "all our [self-] righteous acts are like filthy rags" (Isa. 64:6).

So the answer to the question, "Who goes to heaven?" is the one who believes in Jesus as the Savior and the Christ. Actually, heaven is yet future, when I die. I can't go to heaven before then. But I can have eternal life the moment I believe. Jesus made this claim: "Very truly I tell you, whoever hears my word and believes him who sent me has eternal life and will not be judged but has crossed over from death to life" (John 5:24). He "has" eternal life, not he "will get" eternal life. So in some sense, heaven is here and now—internally, spiritually, personally—and coming later as well.

FOR FURTHER STUDY

John 3:18; 5:46–47; 6:40, 47; 8:24; 9:35–38; 20:29–31; Acts 16:31; Romans 1:16; Ephesians 2:8–9

2 How good must a person be to get to heaven?

When I was in high school, I had an English teacher who gave what seemed to me to be tricky test questions. She wanted the best answer among several answers that were technically all correct. Well, "How good must a person be to get to heaven?" is a question like that. It has two answers. The first answer is the negative, the bad news: no one, not even the very best of us, is good enough to get to heaven.

The Bible is clear that we have all failed God extensively, multiple times. We have repeatedly violated his holy standards, purposefully making self-centered, egocentric choices in what we say and how we live. The apostle Paul in his letter to the Roman Christians repeats numerous times that everyone has committed heinous acts and spoken slanderous words that show how evil we are. "There is no one who is righteous, no one who is wise or who worships God. All have turned away from God; they have all gone wrong; no one does what is right, not even one" (Rom. 3:10–12 TEV). Next Paul highlights how our speech shows this to be true. "Their words are full of deadly deceit; wicked lies roll off their tongues, and dangerous threats, like snake's poison, from their lips; their speech is filled with bitter curses" (Rom. 3:13–14 TEV). The only exception to Paul's universal outlook of people is Jesus. He alone was righteous and without sin (see Heb. 4:15).

But there is another answer to this question. It is this: One has to be as good as Jesus to get to heaven. That doesn't sound like good news, but it is. Let me explain. God doesn't grade on a curve. Even the one who gets a 99 percent score on goodness doesn't get into heaven. Sin is like a cancer. One percent cancer in a vital organ of your body is still a body that is radically unhealthy. And 1 percent sinfulness in a person (if that minimum were even possible!) still makes for an ungodly person. Sin is an addiction, so we do it repeatedly. So how does anyone get as good as Jesus?

The answer is that God declares us to be righteous—just as righteous as Jesus is—when we believe that Jesus is the only one who can forgive us and wipe our slate clean. Like a heavenly bank account that we have far overdrawn, God both cancels our debt (forgiveness) and then deposits a huge payment (justification and eternal life). By placing our faith in Jesus as the only one who can forgive our sin, God looks at us the way he looks at his Son: fully and perfectly Righteous (with a capital R).

Doing good works has nothing to do with getting to heaven. Good works are to be done by the Christian in gratitude that he has already been given eternal life, not in order to get it. Paul said he no longer has "a righteousness of my own from the law, but one that is through faith in Christ—the righteousness from God based on faith" (Phil. 3:9 HCSB). In fact, in order to believe in Jesus Christ in the way Paul describes it ("to the one who does not work," Rom. 4:5), we must abandon all hope of any part of our goodness as contributing in even the smallest way to what Jesus has done for us in his death on the cross and in his resurrection.

If you wanted to become a billionaire but were already in debt by billions of dollars, you would first need to pay off your debt. Then you would need to earn or gain a great amount of wealth. That's what Jesus did for us. First, he paid off our sin debt that was billions in the red with God. But even though that debt was canceled, we still had no wealth or assets. So by faith in Jesus, he put billions into our account. He gives us a righteousness placed in our heavenly bank account that makes us acceptable to God. But what kind of person does God do this for? It is not the person who is good or holy but the ungodly person. Part of believing in Jesus as the only one who can get us to heaven is seeing ourselves as "ungodly." Do you see yourself that way?

Forgiving our sins is certainly part of God's plan to get us to heaven. But it is only part. To "justify" us, God adds something to us. He adds his righteousness to us, declaring us to be completely good in his sight. Receiving God's righteousness also means that we have eternal life. Eternal life is something that we have in the future, but it is also something that we get here and now. It is sometimes difficult for us to understand that eternal life is received as a free gift in this life when we come to faith in Jesus Christ. Someone has said, "Eternal life does not begin with death, it begins with faith."

Jesus said something very similar: "The one who believes in the Son has [right now] eternal life" (John 3:36 HCSB). Eternal life is the present possession of the one who believes, not just a future anticipation. Justification and eternal life come as one package. The one who has eternal life and justification will one day live with Jesus and God forever on the new earth.

Eternal life and justification (being declared righteous even though we aren't fully righteous while on earth) is a free gift. It is not something we get by changing our life or doing good deeds to help others. The Bible makes this clear, even though so many people have twisted the Bible on this subject. Many verses in the New Testament make it clear that acts of kindness do not get us to heaven.

Paul said it over and over again. One expanded Bible translation of Ephesians 2:8–9 says this:

> For it is by free grace (God's unmerited favor) that you are saved (delivered from judgment *and* made partakers of Christ's salvation) through [your] faith. And this [salvation] is not of yourselves [of your own doing, it came not through your own striving], but it is the gift of God; Not because of works [not the fulfillment of the Law's demands], lest any man should boast. [It is not the result of what anyone can possibly do, so no one can pride himself in it or take glory to himself]. (AMP)

The book of Revelation closes out the Bible. Two clear statements about the free gift of life appear in its last two chapters. It is as if God were making a final appeal to everyone to receive Jesus who alone can give the never-ending satisfaction of eternal "water" to the spiritually thirsty person. In the first verse, Jesus himself is talking from heaven. "It is done! I am the Alpha and the Omega, the Beginning and the End. I will give water as a gift to the thirsty from the spring of life" (Rev. 21:6 HCSB). John is the writer in this last remark. "And let the one who is thirsty come; let the one who wants it take the water of life free of charge" (Rev. 22:17 NET).

The message of the New Testament is that God sent his own Son to earth to take on a human body and human nature. The plan was to rescue all humans by punishing his sinless Son, Jesus, on a Roman cross, an ancient method of capital punishment. Jesus was a substitute sacrifice for all people who have ever lived—his undeserved punishment for our deserved punishment. God requires only that one believe in Jesus as the one sent from the Father in heaven as a sacrifice on your behalf.

John 3:16 is probably the most famous verse in the Bible. It tells the good news of eternal life in one sentence. "For God so loved the world that he gave his one and only Son, that whoever believes in him shall not perish but have eternal life."

FOR FURTHER STUDY

Isaiah 55:6–7; John 1:12–13; 6:35; 10:7–9; Romans 4:5; 6:23; Ephesians 2:1–10

3 Do Christians go to heaven immediately after they die?

The simple answer to this question is, "Yes, Christians go to heaven immediately after they die." To one of two thieves who was crucified next to him, Jesus promised, "Today you will be with me in paradise [heaven]" (Luke 23:43). Jesus went to paradise that day, and so did the thief. If the thief went anywhere else after death besides paradise, it was for an extremely short time—half the day was already gone, as they were both put on the cross by noon (v. 44). By the power of Jesus, the thief was destined for paradise immediately after he died. He may have been carried there by angels (Luke 16:22). But keep in mind that *this* heaven is not where we will spend eternity (see question #10).

Next to the apostles, a man named Stephen was one of the earliest leaders in the church at Jerusalem (AD 33–34). Stephen was a man characterized by grace, faith, and the power of the Spirit. He was also the first Christian martyr. While his persecutors were hurling stones at him to put him to death, he cried out, "Lord Jesus, receive my spirit" (Acts 7:59). Did Jesus answer his prayer? Of course! And Stephen fully anticipated that in the next moment Jesus would answer his request and he would be in the presence of the Lord. In fact, every Christian who has truly placed faith in Jesus Christ for his salvation will be transported immediately into heaven like Stephen.

Paul, the great apostle of the Christian church, claimed, "We are confident, I say, and would prefer to be away from the body and at home with the Lord" (2 Cor. 5:8). For Paul and all Christians ("*we* [Christians]") to be away from the body (death) doesn't mean we will be in some ethereal limbo, floating aimlessly in space. Absent from one's body means to be immediately "with the Lord" in heaven. This is the pattern and promise for all of us who have believed in Christ.

Not only was Paul convinced that after death he would immediately be in the presence of the Lord, but he favored being with the Lord in heaven far more than staying on earth. He longed for heaven. Later, he wrote a letter to the Philippian church from a prison in Rome. In his letter, he expressed the possibility that he would be put to death. Death isn't to be dreaded or feared. It means going to heaven. "I am torn between the two," he said. "I desire to depart and be with Christ, which is better by far; but it is more necessary for you that I remain in the body" (Phil. 1:23–24). To "remain in the body" was only desirable for Paul because of the present needs the Philippian Christians had of his guidance and leadership.

Even though heaven was Paul's preference, it never motivated him to commit suicide just to get there. Suicide is a murder of oneself, and murder is against God's moral law. While heaven is "better by far," we don't seek death in ways that displease God. We don't try to kill ourselves or assist others in a premature death. Apart from medical or psychological conditions that render a person incapable of making responsible decisions, suicide is an escape of our problems. Ultimately, Paul desired to stay alive because others needed him. That's selflessness.

By faith, when Christians come in worship and prayer into the presence of God, they are spiritually coming to God in heaven. "But you [believers] have come to Mount Zion, to the city of the living God, the heavenly Jerusalem. You have come to thousands upon thousands of angels in joyful assembly, to the church of the firstborn, whose names are written in heaven. You have come to God, the Judge of all, to the spirits of the righteous made perfect . . ." (Heb. 12:22–23).

The "church of the firstborn" refers to all New Testament believers who have died and are now in heaven. The "firstborn" is Jesus, and the church is his. The "spirits of the righteous made perfect" are the Old Testament believers who died and are now in the presence of Christ in heaven. They were given God's gift of righteousness at the time of faith, just like Abraham (cf. Gen. 15:6; Rom. 4:3). At the death of Jesus, they were made perfect or complete by his sacrifice. Old Testament believers had to await the final pardon of their sins at the cross.

FOR FURTHER STUDY

Psalm 73:24; Ecclesiastes 12:7; John 12:26; 17:24; 1 Thessalonians 4:16–18; Revelation 14:13

4 If people die without Christ, will they get a second chance to go to heaven?

I recently read a story of a man who worked as a high-wire electrician for twenty years. If he touched any one of the wires in his high-voltage environment, he would be electrocuted. And because he typically worked on city high-rise construction projects, the chance of resuscitation after a fall was practically zero. When asked about the risks of this kind of work, he replied, "Well, you don't get a second chance."

Some of life's choices cannot be reversed. Death itself is irreversible, and a woman who has an abortion doesn't get a second chance to revisit that decision. Life is filled with choices that we can't change or alter.

The motivation to see in the Bible the hope of a second chance may be prompted by one's concern for dead loved ones who have not come to faith and may be in hell. Or it may be driven by a misunderstanding of the love of God over against his holiness, righteousness, and justice. But the Bible is clear that one must choose to recognize their sinful condition while alive on earth and place their faith in the death and resurrection of Jesus to forgive their alienation from God. Jesus said that "everyone who has faith in me will live, even if they die" (John 11:25 CEV). Each person must live, and while living he must believe. No one can die and then believe in Jesus.

The central verse that appears to support a second chance for the dead to hear the gospel and gain heaven is 1 Peter 3:19: "After being made alive, he [Jesus] went and made proclamation to the imprisoned spirits." Advocates of a second chance believe that Jesus went into hell to proclaim the good news of the gospel to these dead people. But the next verse continues the same declaration: "[this proclamation was] to those who were disobedient long ago when God waited patiently in the days of Noah."

If this is about a second chance to believe, it is limited to those during the time of Noah and the flood—a small number of all the people throughout history. All Bible interpreters admit that this passage is difficult to understand. One explanation of the passage is that Jesus "made proclamation" of judgment to these imprisoned spirits. He didn't preach the gospel to them. Also, some interpreters believe that Peter is referring to demons, not humans, when he speaks of "the imprisoned spirits." It's best not to create definitive viewpoints based on a single problematic Bible verse.

Another verse used to support the theory of a second chance for salvation after death is in 1 Peter 4:6: "For this is the reason the gospel was preached even to those who are now dead." Here, the simplest understanding is that Peter is referring to Christians who are now dead physically but had received the gospel before death.

In the rest of the Bible, there is certainly no clear suggestion that hope is held out for a second chance. Hebrews 9:27 sets in close sequence our death and our final judgment. "Everyone must die once, and after that be judged by God" (TEV). There is no hint of a second chance here. If we had a second chance to gain heaven after death, then what would motivate us to believe now and to live according to Jesus' teachings?

A second-chance viewpoint suggests that some of those among the dead who have refused to believe in Jesus while alive will do so in the torment of hell. This presumes that their punishment in hell will change their hearts and minds. But nothing in the Bible tells us that anyone's heart will be changed by the experience of hell. When God judges people on earth with various plagues in the final days of human history, the apostle John prophesied that they would not change their hearts. For they "cursed the God of heaven because of their pains and their sores, but they refused to repent of what they had done" (Rev. 16:11). The same will be true of the pains of eternal judgment.

Nothing in the Bible encourages us to think that a person has a second chance to reverse their eternal destiny after death.

FOR FURTHER STUDY

Psalm 78:39; 90:10–12; Matthew 12:32; Mark 3:29; Revelation 9:20–21; 14:10–11; 16:9; 20:10

5 Is heaven the same now as it will be in eternity?

Home has different meanings. When someone asks me, "Where is your home?" I'm not always sure if they mean where I grew up or where I currently live. I grew up in Pennsylvania, but I currently live in Indiana. I also spent two years in California, three years in Oklahoma, four years in Texas, and five years in Illinois. So what you mean by *home* is variable.

Heaven, too, has different meanings. The Bible uses the word *heaven* to mean the sky, the stars, and the planets. It also uses *heaven* to mean where God and Jesus are, and by implication where believing Christians go immediately after we die. Paul tells us that for believers "to be away from the body" (i.e., to die) is to be "at home with the Lord" (2 Cor. 5:8). But many people, including Christians, also use the word *heaven* to mean where people will spend eternity. This is not wrong. But in actuality, those who have believed in Jesus will spend eternity on a new earth. We won't be floating on clouds.

Peter wrote, "God has promised us a . . . new earth, where justice will rule. We are really looking forward to that!" (2 Peter 3:13 CEV).

The old earth will be radically reformed to become a perfect, sinless earth. This takes place in the future when "the heavens will pass away with a roar and the elements will be destroyed with intense heat, and the earth and its works will be burned up" (v. 10 NASB). (For more about the new earth, see question #10.)

So when Christians speak of going to heaven, we are speaking of going to a temporary location until the new earth is created. Bible interpreters often call this temporary place for believers "the intermediate heaven." Our final place of happiness is not actually called *heaven* in the Bible because God's dwelling place (heaven) will come down to be united with a newly created *earth*. The apostle John speaks of how an angel showed him this event, "And he carried me away in the Spirit . . . and showed me the Holy City, Jerusalem, coming down out of heaven from God" (Rev. 21:10). This re-created "Jerusalem" will be placed on the new earth. Heaven and earth will become one.

The intermediate heaven is like a temporary place of transition until the end of the world and eternity begins. The final "heaven"—the new earth—will be brought about after our body is resurrected, the final judgment takes place, and the old heaven and earth are destroyed. At the resurrection, true followers of Christ will receive a resurrected body to join with their disembodied spirit (or soul). God will then re-create the old earth into a new "resurrected" earth. Eternity is really heaven on earth.

Believers will personally be with Jesus in both the temporary heaven and the eternal "heaven," the new earth. The Bible makes this promise, "And so we will be with the Lord forever" (1 Thess. 4:17). There are no differences in the fellowship and companionship believers will have with the Lord in these two "heavens," or of the happiness they will experience.

What then are the differences? In the intermediate heaven, we will not have a resurrected body. Some think we will have a temporary body until we get our final, resurrected body. They suggest that in the Bible, the souls described in heaven wear clothes (white robes), can be seen by others, have voices that cry out, etc. John wrote in Revelation that he saw "the souls of those who had been slain because of the word of God. . . . They called out in a loud voice, 'How long, Sovereign Lord, holy and true, until you judge the inhabitants of the earth and avenge our blood?' Then each of them was given a white robe. . . ." (Rev. 6:9–11).

Others suggest that Paul views death as a time when believers are "unclothed," i.e., without a body. Here on earth, while we wait for our final home (our resurrection body), "we groan, longing to be clothed instead with our heavenly dwelling [our resurrected body], because when we are clothed, we will not be found naked . . ." (2 Cor. 5:2–3). Paul's comment about being temporarily "naked" might imply that we will be without a body in the temporary heaven.

In the temporary heaven, believers will rest from their earthly labors. There will be no need to share the gospel with others, or to help the poor and needy, or to be diligent to earn a living, or to do other responsibilities Jesus commands of us in earthly life. In the eternal heaven, with a resurrected body, we will carry on some responsibilities again for the Lord. (See question #12.)

FOR FURTHER STUDY

Matthew 27:52–53; John 14:23; Acts 7:59; Romans 8:21; 1 Corinthians 15:42–44; Revelation 21:1–3

6 Is Jesus in heaven right now?

Nothing is more central to Christianity than the resurrection of Jesus. A Christian's faith is totally dependent on it. And nothing is more exclusive to the Christian's faith as well. No other reputable religious leader of any other major religion claims to have died and been raised back to life.

Although his followers never caught on until after his resurrection, Jesus predicted many times that he would die a violent death on a cross and be raised from the dead three days later (cf. Mark 8:31; John 12:32–33). But he also predicted that after the resurrection he would go back into heaven to be with the Father (cf. John 7:33; 13:3; 16:28). So his resurrection and ascension are closely tied together.

For forty more days after the resurrection, Jesus lived on the earth in a resurrected body, met with his disciples several times, and appeared to many followers. Paul said that on one occasion Jesus appeared to at least five hundred people all at once (1 Cor. 15:6). At the end of the forty days, he was taken up into heaven.

Luke, an early follower of Christ and a physician by trade, wrote down one of the accounts of Jesus' life (the gospel of Luke). In a second book, the book of Acts, he recounted how followers, especially Paul, spread the church during the first thirty years following Jesus' resurrection. Luke says that in a small town called Bethany, "While he [Jesus] was blessing them [the disciples], he left them and was taken up into heaven" (Luke 24:51).

In Acts, Luke recorded the same event with more detail. Jesus was

taken up before their very eyes, and a cloud hid him from their sight. They were looking intently up into the sky as he was going, when suddenly two men [angels] dressed in white stood beside them. "Men of Galilee," they said, "why do you stand here looking into the sky? This same Jesus, who has been taken from you into heaven, will come back in the same way you have seen him go into heaven" (1:9–11).

So what is Jesus doing in heaven? First, he sat down at God's right hand. Sitting down symbolizes the fact that Jesus has finished all the work he needs to do to accomplish our forgiveness. Like the priests of the Old Testament who brought sacrifices into the

27

earthly temple, Jesus brought himself into the heavenly temple as the definitive, end-all sacrifice.

Second, while in heaven, Jesus is preparing eternal residences or homes for all who have believed. The night before his crucifixion, he told his disciples, "My Father's house has many rooms; if that were not so, would I have told you that I am going there to prepare a place for you?" (John 14:2). God doesn't need to prepare anything. He can just create it. So a place that Jesus will "prepare" for us suggests its quality, beauty, comfort, and more. Jesus was a carpenter on earth. But his heavenly carpentry skills will exceed all comparisons.

Third, Jesus is in heaven waiting. He is waiting for the time when the Father tells him to defeat his enemies—those who have refused to believe that he is Lord and King. "But when this priest [Jesus] had offered for all time one sacrifice for sins, he sat down at the right hand of God, and since that time he waits for his enemies to be made his footstool" (Heb. 10:12–13). The Old Testament promised that the Messiah would one day sit at God's right hand and ultimately defeat all his enemies (Ps. 110:1). Shortly after Jesus' ascension, Peter told a large audience that this Old Testament prophecy was fulfilled by Jesus (Acts 2:34–35).

Finally, from his place seated at God's right hand—a position of highest honor—Jesus will return to earth at the Father's command to reign as king over the world. At this point, he will destroy all the ungodly on earth and bring in the final resurrection.

Right before his death as a martyr, Stephen said that he miraculously saw "heaven open and the Son of Man standing at the right hand of God" (Acts 7:56). Jesus was not sitting but standing! Perhaps Jesus stands up to welcome into heaven all those who have been his faithful followers.

FOR FURTHER STUDY

Mark 12:35–37; 14:62; Luke 9:51; Acts 2:32–33; 1 Thessalonians 1:10; 4:16; Hebrews 4:14; Revelation 1:12–18; 3:21

7 What did Jesus mean by "mansions" in heaven?

A story is told of a little girl who was about to walk through a cemetery. She was asked by a stranger if she was afraid. "No," she replied. "My home is on the other side." Home. For most of us, *home* is a nice-sounding word. It's the place where we feel at ease, comfortable, and secure.

A Christian's eternal home will be in heaven. But what kind of home will that be? Is it a mansion? The King James Version of the Bible, first printed in 1611, reads, "In my Father's house are many mansions: if it were not so, I would have told you. I go to prepare a place for you" (John 14:2).

I scanned the Internet and found the top ten mega-mansions in the United States. One was built for $50 million but sold for only $11.5 million in 2011. Three others were currently on the market. That's what happens with earthly homes. The residents eventually move out, sometimes by death. The mansions ranged from 36,000 to 100,000 square feet. Most of us don't need and couldn't use that much personal space. Do we each need a personal bowling alley and an Olympic-size swimming pool?

In the English of the time the KJV was written, the original meaning of the word *mansion* meant simply "dwelling," not a large, luxurious house. Unfortunately, the idea of mansions in heaven has become an enduring tradition in some Christian circles. It can be found in popular hymns and songs such as the Southern Gospel favorite, "I've Got a Mansion Just Over the Hilltop."

As a result, many have pictured heaven as consisting of huge estates or even castles where we will live. But modern translations render John 14:2, "My Father's house has many rooms," "many dwelling places" (HCSB), or "many places to live in" (NJB). Don't

29

think of "rooms" as small apartments, hotel rooms, or dormitory rooms! The many rooms or living quarters in the Father's house are suggestive of the spacious provisions for each person and the incredible number of people who will use them.

The original word for *rooms* was sometimes used outside the Bible for a place of rest after a long journey. The word implied a place where someone would stay or remain—a more permanent stopping place. Our earthly journey will end in a wonderful rest in God's house in heaven, and there we will stay forever.

Jesus told the disciples that he was going to his Father's house in heaven "to prepare a place for you." Jesus described our home in the Father's house as a "place." A "place" is something physical, not an idea or a state of mind. And when Jesus said, "that where I am" (v. 3), he was referring to a place, a location, not a transcendent nothingness. Heaven will have physical characteristics, just as his resurrected body has physical characteristics.

In ancient Jewish culture, after a wedding it was customary for the groom to take his new bride to an extension that he had built onto his father's house during their engagement. American culture might consider this unacceptable, but it was economically wise to them. The New Testament often uses the image of Jesus as our bridegroom and his people as his bride. The words in John 14:2, "many rooms," say nothing about the size of the rooms—or, better, the living quarters. But what bridegroom, in building a home or living quarters for his bride, would not do all he could to make it both attractive and comfortable? Will Jesus, the bridegroom, do less than that?

The Father's house is heaven, where God resides. Our home is wherever he lives. The final living quarters for us will be in the new Jerusalem (see question #22) on the new earth (see question #21). God will come to live with us there.

FOR FURTHER STUDY

John 12:26; 13:33–36; 14:1–6; 17:24; 2 Corinthians 5:1; Hebrews 11:9–16; 13:14; Revelation 3:12–13

8 Do people in heaven know what is happening on earth?

I t has been said that a secret sin on earth is an open scandal in heaven. That may be true. We know from the Bible that the angels are watching and know what we do (1 Cor. 4:9). They are even called "watchers" (Dan. 4:13, 17, 23 ESV). But are people who have died and are in heaven also watching? Nothing clearly says they are able to see what is happening. But several Bible passages seem to imply that they might somehow know what is happening. Does God tell them?

One fascinating vision is in Revelation 6. John explained, "I saw under the altar [of the temple in heaven] the souls of those who had been slain because of the word of God and the testimony they had maintained." These men and women were martyred for their faith. John continued, "They called out in a loud voice, 'How long, Sovereign Lord, holy and true, until you judge the inhabitants of the earth and avenge our blood?'" (6:9–10). It is interesting that their identity had not changed in heaven. They were martyrs on earth. They will be known as martyrs in heaven. In their heavenly existence, they remember their lives on earth, particularly that they were murdered. They are fully aware that their persecutors on earth have not yet been judged by God. So they cry out to him to bring about justice on the earth.

Jesus often spent time with immoral and unethical people. The religious leaders usually grumbled about his association with such people. Jesus replied to such criticism, "There will be more rejoicing in heaven over one sinner who repents than over ninety-nine righteous persons who do not need to repent" (Luke 15:7). He repeated his challenge: "There is rejoicing in the presence of the angels of God over one sinner who repents" (v. 10). Angels see the people on earth who repent, and participate in a celebration for them. But the rejoicing is "in the presence of the angels." Apparently, Christians in heaven also know when someone comes to faith, and they join in with rejoicing.

After the prophet Samuel died, the Israelite king named Saul disobeyed God's command and sought out a female medium to reveal the outcome of Israel's impending battle with their enemy, the Philistines. He demanded the medium call up Samuel from the dead. Mediums don't really channel dead people but rather evil spirits impersonating dead people. So when Samuel himself actually spoke in their presence, the medium was utterly shocked.

In Samuel's message from the dead, he remembered what had happened before he had died: He had given Saul a prophecy that the Lord would hand over the kingdom of Israel to David because of Saul's rebellion. Now in the afterlife, he knew that prophecy was coming true (1 Sam. 28:4–19).

Hundreds of years later, on an unknown mountain, Jesus was physically transformed into a brilliant appearance while three of his disciples looked on. "Suddenly two men were there talking with him. They were Moses and Elijah, who appeared in heavenly glory and talked with Jesus about the way in which he would soon fulfill God's purpose by dying in Jerusalem" (Luke 9:30–31 TEV). These men had been Old Testament prophets. But they were fully aware of Jesus' upcoming death.

How did they know this about Jesus or even know who he was? Perhaps they had listened in from heaven and learned from Jesus' earthly messages. Or perhaps God told them directly while they were in heaven. But make note of this. There is nothing that we will learn about events on earth that will destroy the joy of heaven.

On one occasion, Jesus told the Jewish religious leaders about two men who knew each other in life (Luke 16:19–31). One was a beggar who had physical disabilities. His name was Lazarus. At death, he was carried by angels to a place of great comfort. There he was able to begin a wonderful friendship with Abraham, the dead patriarch of the Jews.

It is even possible that people in hell know some things that are happening on earth. The other man was very rich and lived in luxury every day. Although in life the poor man begged at the rich man's gate, the rich man apparently ignored him. After his death, the wealthy man went to Hades (see question #34), or hell. A great chasm separated the place of torment where the rich man was and the place of comfort where Abraham and the poor man were. Yet in his torment the rich man was able to call out to Abraham, "Send Lazarus to my family, for I have five brothers. Let him warn them, so that they will not also come to this place of torment" (vv. 16:27–28). How did the rich man know that his five brothers were still alive? We are unsure. But it's logical to assume from his remark that he knew something of what was happening on earth with his five brothers.

FOR FURTHER STUDY

2 Samuel 28:16–19; Luke 9:28–36; 1 Corinthians 4:9; 1 Timothy 3:16; Hebrews 12:1; Revelation 18:20; 19:1–5, 11–14

9 What does the Old Testament say about heaven?

Parents don't unload complex information on their young children. How to invest in stocks is not explained to a child, but parents may teach them how to spend and how to save. God follows a similar pattern. He gradually discloses truth. The Old Testament was more about how God could come down to connect with people through a temple. In the New Testament, Jesus replaces the temple (cf. John 2:19–22). He is the final "place" where people commune with God. When he died, was resurrected, and ascended to heaven, more truth was given about how we go to be with him in heaven after death. Through Jesus' teachings and those of the apostles, God clarified several less-developed truths given in the Old Testament.

It's not surprising, then, that the Old Testament has much less information about heaven than the New Testament. But several truths about heaven are still revealed there. First, in numerous Old Testament passages, God and his angels are said to live in heaven. Jacob, the grandson of Abraham, "had a dream in which he saw a stairway resting on the earth, with its top reaching to heaven, and the angels of God were ascending and descending on it" (Gen. 28:12). In awe and wonder, Jacob called what he saw "the gate of heaven" (v. 17). The psalmist cried out to the Lord, "Whom have I in heaven but you?" (Ps. 73:25).

Second, the Old Testament had a concept of bodily resurrection. The resurrection for Old Testament believers was also thought to be eternal. In a dream of the future, a heavenly being that looked like a man dressed in linen (Dan. 10:5, 16) gave a long message to Daniel. In his concluding remarks, he declared, "Multitudes who sleep in the dust of the earth will awake: some to everlasting life, others to shame and everlasting contempt" (Dan. 12:2). That the faithful Jews of the Old Testament believed in a bodily resurrection is confirmed by the Jewish woman Martha in the New Testament. After her brother, Lazarus, died, Martha told Jesus, "I know he will rise again in the resurrection at the last day" (John 11:24).

Third, this resurrection meant being with God himself. One of the Jerusalem temple musicians wrote, "God will redeem me from the realm of the dead; he will surely take me *to himself*" (italics added, Ps. 49:15). Job had this confidence too. In what is perhaps the oldest book of the Bible, Job affirmed, "After my skin has been destroyed, yet in my flesh I will see God; I myself will see him with my own eyes—I, and not another. How my heart yearns within me!" (Job 19:26–27).

In Genesis, the first book of the Bible, we are told that "Enoch walked faithfully with God; then he was no more, because God took him away" (5:24). The implication is that Enoch escaped a natural, physical death and that he was taken to be with God in heaven. Elijah, the Old Testament prophet, was also taken by God in a whirlwind to heaven without seeing death (2 Kings 2:1, 11).

Fourth, Old Testament people of faith believed that one day they would live in an eternal land and an eternal city. The Jewish writer of the New Testament book of Hebrews explains that the men and women of faith in the Old Testament thought of themselves as foreigners and strangers on earth. This is one of the reasons that many of the patriarchs of the Jewish people lived in tents. They "were longing for a better country—a heavenly one" (Heb. 11:16). Tents don't have much of a foundation. Abraham, Isaac, and Jacob were "looking forward to the city with foundations, whose architect and builder is God" (v. 10).

In the Old Testament, first the tabernacle and then the temple was where God said he would personally meet with his people (Ex. 25:22). In the temple, the priests could have delightful fellowship with God. In the most famous psalm of the Bible, David wrote, "Surely your goodness and love will follow me all the days of my life, and I will dwell in the house of the LORD forever" (Ps. 23:6). David did not mean that he desired to live eternally inside the earthly temple in Jerusalem. His longing was to live in God's presence forever. Jesus is our temple, and the new Jerusalem is our city with foundations (see question #22).

FOR FURTHER STUDY

Genesis 2:9; Deuteronomy 4:39; 1 Samuel 2:6; 2 Samuel 12:23; 2 Kings 2:1–12; Psalm 16:9–11; 17:15; Daniel 2:28; Acts 23:6–8

10 What does the Bible mean by the "new earth"?

I'm one of those people who has a hard time getting rid of left-over or broken items. If it is something I think I can fix or use later, it's hard for me to part with it. I'm always asking, *Can I use this piece of wood on another project? What if I need this strip of metal someday?* So I have to exercise painful self-discipline to get rid of these "valuable" stockpiles of "useful" materials.

God doesn't like to throw out anything either. He's in the business of restoring, renovating, and renewing his creation. In the future, he intends to dramatically recycle the old heavens and the old earth as we know them, not just eliminate them completely. God spoke through the Old Testament prophet Isaiah, "See, I will create new heavens [the stars, etc.] and a new earth. The former things will not be remembered, nor will they come to mind" (Isa. 65:17). "Heaven" is not actually the final destiny of the believing Christian. The new earth is our ultimate eternal home. But Christians speak of "going to heaven" because that is where we go when we die. The new heavens and new earth have not been created yet. The old heavens and old earth will be destroyed first. The apostle John foresaw in a vision the end of this earth as we know it. He saw "a new heaven and a new earth," when "the first heaven and the first earth had passed away, and there was no longer any sea" (Rev. 21:1).

Present-day oceans ("sea") came about as a result of the judgment of the flood during the days of Noah (Gen. 6–8). In the Old Testament era, the oceans were always a threat to human life (and are still today). The sea was frequently portrayed as a symbol of unrest, violence, and danger. So the new earth will only have bodies of fresh water. Currently, 70 percent of the earth's surface is covered by oceans, containing 98 percent of all the water on the earth. But the ocean, which has little function for most of human life, will disappear. There will be no evidence of judgment on the new earth.

The central city on the new earth will be the new Jerusalem (see question #22). But nothing else is told to us precisely in the Bible about the size, appearance, or composition of the new earth. Since the final place of eternal living for the followers of Christ will be on a new earth, we can assume that there will be much continuity with the old earth. Why call it the new *earth* unless the Bible wants us to think of a connection to this earth? We can imagine the new earth will be much like the old, but exceptionally more beautiful. I expect to see forests, grass, flowers, animals, waterfalls, mountains, and more.

Some Bible passages speak of the new earth as a garden of Eden, recalling God's original garden creation for the very first two people before sin entered the world. At that time, there were no devouring insects, blight, drought, floods, or forest fires. Nor will there be on the new earth. Speaking of the future Jerusalem on the new earth, the prophet Isaiah said that the Lord "will make her deserts like Eden, her wastelands like the garden of the LORD" (Isa. 51:3).

The Sahara desert in North Africa, almost the size of the United States, will disappear. The ice-free areas of Antarctica (South Pole) and the Artic (North Pole) are considered polar deserts; their vegetation cannot support human life. Yet such desert areas will become places that yield vibrant plant life and streams of water to sustain this new foliage. In every place on the new earth, water essential for all life will be in abundance.

Jesus promised that in a future day, he will proclaim from his throne, "I am making everything new." Then he told John to write down, "these words are trustworthy and true" (Rev. 21:5). Jesus also spoke of a time when, "at the renewal of all things, when the Son of Man sits on his glorious throne," his disciples would also rule with him (Matt. 19:28). The apostle Peter explained to a large gathering of fellow Jews about the resurrection and ascension of

Jesus, "Heaven must receive him until the time comes for God to restore everything, as he promised long ago through his holy prophets" (Acts 3:21).

FOR FURTHER STUDY

Isaiah 32:14–15; 65:17; 66:22; Romans 8:20–22; 2 Peter 3:7, 10–13; Revelation 21:1; 22:1

11 What will we do in heaven?

Dwight Moody, the great evangelist, was the Billy Graham of the late nineteenth century. He tells a story in one of his books about a young girl whose mother was deathly sick. A neighbor took the child next door for the mother so that the young girl would not watch her mother die. The neighbor did not even allow the child to attend her own mother's funeral. Finally, the girl was allowed back in her home. She ran from room to room, looking for her mother. But when she was told that her mother had passed away, she cried out to the neighbor, "Take me back to your house! I don't want to be here if my mother isn't here."

Moody concluded, "It wasn't the home that made it so sweet to the child. It was the presence of her mother. And so it is not heaven alone that is attractive to us. It is that Jesus, our loving Savior, is there." Whatever we do in heaven, we will be doing it with Jesus.

For one thing, we won't be doing anything evil or sinful. In this present life we sometimes lie, cheat, are greedy, gossip, and criticize others. The book of Revelation lists several of the many devastating things that are totally absent from our experience in heaven and the new earth (21:4; 22:3, 5): death, mourning, weeping, pain, disappointment, failures, and the curse on nature and the earth (like weeds in our garden and the death of animals). So whatever we do, it will be done in happiness and joy. Many good fairy tales end, "And they lived happily ever after." That's really a description of heaven, not earth.

Being around Jesus will be more exciting than we can imagine. Jesus said there would be laughter in heaven too. "Blessed are you who weep now, for you will laugh" (Luke 6:21). Martin Luther, leader of the Protestant Reformation, once said, "If you are not allowed to laugh in heaven, I don't want to go there."

For all eternity, heaven will be a continuing experience of new adventures that will bring us into community and unbroken friendships with others. Mark Twain said facetiously, "What a man misses mostly in heaven is company." He was far from the truth. We will make friends with millions of people in heaven, one by one, without the worry of conflicts or estrangements. They will become like intimate family members or best friends. There will be no issues with quirks and idiosyncrasies we've had on earth. No shyness, embarrassments, or fears of looking bad. No inadequate articulation, no speech inadequacies or impediments, no thoughts of being unattractive, too tall or too short, too fat or too thin.

God knows all things and is infinitely creative. He will never stop creating. It's part of who God is—the Creator. He created the world with its millions of intricate creatures, peoples, and plants. In the future, he will create a new heaven and a new earth. We have been made in God's image (Gen. 1:26–27). Our very nature is to be creative too. Life in heaven will continue this creativity. The artist on earth will create art in heaven that will give glory to God. We will join in worship as we see her artwork. The musician in this life will continue to create new music in heaven with which we will sing praises to our God. The musicians will be unable to exhaust the possibilities of new music for all eternity. New instruments with new musical sounds will be invented regularly.

Heaven will involve eternal discovery and learning. So there will be eternal opportunities for the scientist and others to discover God's creations and lead us in worship of God's marvelous powers and wisdom. Learning will be inexhaustible and unending. Teachers will be needed to explain to others God's never-ending phenomena as they are discovered. Routine excitement about new heavenly discoveries will make the thrill of our newest technological toy on earth seem pathetic.

Above all, we will worship God and Jesus in heaven, often with singing. In heaven, God and Jesus will be the center of attention. Have you ever looked at a sunset and marveled at God's handiwork? What was that feeling like? Awe, amazement, wonder! That's what it will be like to continually honor and worship God in heaven. Some worship will be directed and formal; some will be spontaneous and informal. In heaven, we will have everything we want, and we will want everything we have. In heaven, we will do everything we want, and we will want to do everything we do. For this, we will praise God.

FOR FURTHER STUDY

Psalm 16:11; Isaiah 51:11; 55:12; 65:17–18; Zechariah 2:10; Matthew 25:14–30; Hebrews 12:22–23; Revelation 5:13; 22:3

12 Will we have to work in heaven?

When I was young, I resisted doing work assigned to me by my father. Few children actually like to do chores. Even the word *chores* carries negative overtones. Any child would rather play than do chores. Nevertheless, in the summers, my father assigned me to mow the yard and weed the vegetable garden at our home. Ironically, today I do the same things at my home and garden. But now I actually enjoy some of this work that I do. Among the many things we will do in heaven is work, but we will thoroughly enjoy it. Work in heaven will not be like most work on earth. Work in heaven will be without difficulty, frustration, drudgery, purposelessness, or monotony. " 'Difficulty' is not a word to be found in the dictionary of heaven," wrote C. H. Spurgeon. Instead, work in heaven will be radically fulfilling, even fun. God will assign us individual tasks and responsibilities.

We were never created to be inactive, even in heaven. Work was always part of God's creation for people. In the beginning, God himself worked in creative activity for six days when he made the world (Gen. 2:2–3). Jesus also worked. In a prayer to the Father, he said, "I have brought you glory on earth by finishing the work you gave me to do" (John 17:4). Work itself is not a curse or punishment. But the sin of Adam and Eve brought about a new kind of work as part of the punishment for sin. Work was now more difficult, painful, and less productive than it should have been. It brought sweat, fatigue, and toil never intended for us by our Creator. Work can be very fulfilling. Some people actually have jobs on earth that they thoroughly enjoy. Our work in heaven will be to serve the Lord Jesus.

In heaven, God's "servants will serve him" (Rev. 22:3). A servant is one who does work for another. Our heavenly service will be deeply satisfying, always agreeable, and without exhaustion or tiredness, without pressures or failures. With the absence of these negative concerns, we will be able to serve God continually and joyfully. A group of martyrs in heaven seen in a vision by the apostle John are said to "serve him [God] day and night" (7:15).

One of many tasks given out will be leadership responsibilities. In one parable, Jesus taught that his faithful followers would rule over cities in the world to come. Ones who are more faithful will receive more cities to rule over (Luke 19:17–19). (For more details, see question #49.) There will be a need for administrators, leaders, managers, directors, etc. In another parable, Jesus explained how a master went on a trip, returned, and found that his servant was

41

faithful in his absence. "Truly I tell you, he will put him in charge of all his possessions" (Luke 12:44). Obviously, the master in the parable was the Lord Jesus himself. He will assign these positions in the world to come. In eternity, the new heavens and the new earth and all that is in them will be God's possessions. We can become those who will rule over God's possessions, including the exercise of leadership over the angels. Paul asked the Corinthian Christians rhetorically, "Do you not know that we will judge [i.e., rule] angels?" (1 Cor. 6:3).

When I was young, I used to resist going to bed early just like I resisted doing work around the house. Few children actually like to go to bed. It's more fun to stay up and play. But when I got older, going to bed was both needed and welcome. The word *rest* sounded pretty good at the end of the day. Heaven is also a time of rest. In one of John's visions, he was told to write, "Blessed are the dead who die in the Lord. . . . They will rest from their labor" (Rev. 14:13). God rested on the seventh day after creation, but this was not because he was tired. His rest showed that his work was completed. In heaven, we will complete many tasks assigned to us by God, and then we will rest. Rest in heaven will include times to eat, drink, and celebrate with our Lord (see question #32). Jesus promised, "Come to me, all you who are weary and burdened, and I will give you rest" (Matt. 11:28). That promise is for now, and forever.

FOR FURTHER STUDY

Genesis 2:1–3; Luke 16:10; John 4:34; 2 Timothy 2:12; Hebrews 2:5–9; 4:3–6; Revelation 11:15; 22:5

13 What will heaven look like?

Greenland has nine times the suicide rate of the United States per capita and leads the countries of the world in this tragedy. In the United States, Alaska has more suicides per capita than any other state. One contributing factor may be the lack of daylight hours in these regions of the world. In Barrow, Alaska, at the very top of the state, the sun never rises during two months of the winter. Darkness can be very depressing, while sunshine can be tremendously cheerful. Sunlight is essential for all life.

John was charged with writing down a vision of the future. He described the future new Jerusalem (see question #22)—where the followers of Jesus will live in eternity—as a city that "does not need the sun or the moon to shine on it, for the glory of God gives it light, and the Lamb [Jesus] is its lamp. The nations will walk by its light. . . . On no day will its gates ever be shut, for there will be no night there" (Rev. 21:23–25).

Barrow, Alaska, has eighty-five continuous days of daylight in the summer. But in heaven it will be "daylight" all the time. This is true of the intermediate heaven and the eternal "heaven," the new earth. (For details about what the new earth will look like, see question #10.) John repeated this idea of the future light in heaven later in Revelation. "There will be no more night. They will not need the light of a lamp or the light of the sun, for the Lord God will give them light" (22:5). No night! No darkness! Perhaps there will be no need for sleep either. Whether we think of the intermediate heaven, where believers go after death, or the eternal "heaven"—the new earth—there is sure to be plenty of cheerful brightness coming from the radiance of God and Christ.

Much of the Bible implies that heaven and the new earth are so astounding that our words may not be capable of describing them adequately. Paul wrote, " 'What no eye has seen, what no ear has heard, and what no human mind has conceived'—the things God has prepared for those who love him" (1 Cor. 2:9). He was speaking not only about what God has done for his people in the present time (e.g., salvation) but also about what awaits them in eternity. On another occasion, Paul said that there was a time he "was caught up to paradise and heard inexpressible things, things that no one is permitted to tell" (2 Cor. 12:4). Not only the sights, but even the sounds of heaven must be astounding. Perhaps in our sinful condition on earth we are incapable of fathoming the ultimate glory and beauty of God in heaven.

One visible picture of heaven in all its descriptions is the throne of God and the encircling angels there. When John saw heaven in his vision, he "heard the voice of many angels, numbering thousands upon thousands, and ten thousand times ten thousand. They encircled the throne [of God] . . ." (Rev. 5:11). Expect to see angels in heaven, and lots of them. In several of John's visions, he spoke with angels (17:1; 21:9). We can assume that we too will talk with angels in heaven. We may discover in discussions with angels how they helped other believers we know, or even how they helped us personally.

There are also strange-looking heavenly beings that God has created that we will see in heaven. For example, the Bible speaks a few times of seraphim (plural; the singular is seraph). They are described as standing upright and having three pairs of wings, as well as human faces and hands. Cherubim, another group of heavenly creatures, are described as ones who serve in the very presence of God. They seem to have a winged human-animal form.

Four "living creatures" appear in the book of Revelation. They have the faces of a lion, ox, man, and eagle respectively. "Each of the four living creatures had six wings and was covered with eyes all around, even under its wings" (Rev. 4:8). So keep in mind that all the looks and shapes of creatures that God has created are not on this earth. All of these heavenly creatures worship the Creator God continually. (On seeing God in heaven, see question #25.)

FOR FURTHER STUDY

Genesis 3:24; Exodus 37:7–9; Psalm 11:4; Isaiah 6:1–8; 37:16; 60:19–20; Ezekiel 10; Hebrews 1:14; Revelation 4–5

14 Where is heaven?

Perhaps this question sounds rather silly. Heaven is high up in space, isn't it? But what if two people are on different sides of the globe? Then where is heaven? Dwight L. Moody, the great evangelist of the late 1800s, said, "We talk about heaven being so far away. It is within speaking distance to those who belong there."

Actually, the Bible speaks of three "heavens" in a similar way to how we use the word. The *first* heaven is our atmosphere where the birds fly and from where the clouds give us our rain. The *second* heaven is outer space, the place of the stars and planets in the universe. When God speaks of creating the "heavens and the earth" in Genesis, the first book of the Bible, he is talking mostly about the universe and the galaxies of space. But when we say that a family member who knows the Lord has gone to heaven, we are speaking of a place of great happiness in the very presence of God. This is the *third* heaven. This heaven is not the permanent place for those who have believed in Jesus as the Messiah (i.e., the Christ). This is a temporary place we call "heaven," but it is not our final, eternal home. Some Christians call it "the present heaven" or "the intermediate heaven."

Our final "heaven" is actually on earth. That may be surprising, but it's true. God is in the business of renovating, restoring, remaking, regenerating, resurrecting, and many other good actions like that which begin with re-. He is not one to discard and destroy without cause or purpose. So he fully intends—and promises—to remake the old earth into a new earth. That is the final "heaven" for all who have come to faith in Christ. That is why the "heaven" to which a believer in Jesus goes when he or she dies is not their final, eternal home. God has not yet made our final, eternal heaven—the new earth. We can go to live with God and Jesus in the temporary heaven even though we do not yet have a resurrected body. But for the new earth, the final "heaven," we will need a resurrected body, which the Lord will give to us. We will receive this body at the final stages of world history when Jesus returns.

The temporary heaven and the eternal heaven are somewhat different. We call both of these places "heaven" because in each of them God himself will be there. Right now, God is in heaven. Have you heard the prayer that Jesus taught his disciples to pray? It is sometimes called the Lord's Prayer. It begins, "Our Father who is in heaven . . ." (Matt. 6:9 NASB). God is in heaven, but so is Jesus since the time he was lifted up to heaven forty days after his resurrection. Two angels told the disciples who were watching him go, "Why stand looking into the sky? This same Jesus who has been taken up from you into Heaven will come in just the same way as you have seen Him going into Heaven" (Acts 1:11 WEYMOUTH).

So we can see from this passage that heaven is up, but it isn't absolutely clear what "up" means, since God is not limited to our dimensions. Heaven may also be much closer than we think, but in a realm invisible to us. There are several places in the Bible that describe how God opened up heaven for someone to see. Stephen, the first believer who was martyred in the newly formed New Testament church, saw heaven opened. He was about to be killed by some of his fellow Jews. But filled with strength by the Spirit of God, he gazed into heaven and saw God's glory. "Look!" he said.

"I see the heavens opened and the Son of Man standing at the right hand of God!" (Acts 7:56 NKJV). If Stephen could see heaven, Jesus, and God the Father in his vision, they may be closer than we imagine. Perhaps heaven is close, but just in another dimension that we cannot see unless God "opens" it for us.

Several Old Testament prophets had visions of heaven: Elisha, Isaiah, Ezekiel, and Daniel. Elisha saw his predecessor, Elijah, taken "up to heaven" (2 Kings 2:11). The "heavens were opened" to Ezekiel (Ezek. 1:1), and he saw the throne room of the Lord. Daniel had a vision he describes this way: "I kept looking in the night visions, and behold, with the clouds of heaven One like a Son of Man was coming. And He came up to the Ancient of Days and was presented before Him" (Dan. 7:13 NASB). The "Son of Man" is Jesus before he took on a human body. In Daniel's vision, the Son of Man was "riding" the clouds, so to speak. The "Ancient of Days" refers to God the Father.

The amazing fact is that the final "heaven," the new earth, is the future place that God will live too. God, of course, does not need a physical place to stay. His very nature is to be eternally everywhere at once. But he often displays himself in a specific place and time. He has chosen to be visibly present with us on the new earth. In other words, instead of our going up to live with God somewhere, he will come down to live with us! In the book of Revelation, John wrote about a vision he had of this future event. "Then I saw a new heaven and a new earth, for the first heaven and earth had ceased to exist. . . . And I heard a loud voice from the throne saying: 'Look! The residence of God is among human beings. He will live among them, and they will be his people, and God himself will be with them'" (21:1, 3 NET).

So where is the temporary or intermediate heaven where those who have believed in Jesus go after death? The Bible says that it is in the presence of Jesus. Paul wrote that as believers, "we know that when this earthly tent we live in is taken down (that is, when we die and leave this earthly body), we will have a house in heaven, an eternal body made for us by God himself. . . . Yes, we are fully confident, and we would rather be away from these earthly bodies, for then we will be at home with the Lord" (2 Cor. 5:1, 8 NLT).

FOR FURTHER STUDY

Isaiah 14:12–15; 65:17–19; Joel 3:17–21; Revelation 14:1–3, 14–16; 21:1–27

15 Will animals be in heaven?

I once saw a sign that said, "The more I get to know people, the more I love my dog." This is probably not a surprising sentiment to animal lovers—pets can be more loyal and loving than people sometimes. Over the years we've had three Labrador retrievers with four litters of puppies, with sixteen puppies in one of the litters! You don't know fun until you've been surrounded by sixteen puppies all trying to lick your face.

My wife has also owned horses most of our married life. All this to say, we love animals. And over the years, the death of the dogs and horses we've had as pets (not to mention our kids' guinea pigs) hurt us deeply. So I understand why the question of whether or not animals will be in heaven is important to people.

Of course animals are not the same as people, regardless of what some animal-rights advocates think. People have an eternal soul or spirit (and a resurrected body) that goes on forever beyond the grave. People must face the eternal God who will judge every person for how he or she has lived, spoken, thought, and desired. The key issue will be whether a person has his or her name listed in the "Book of Life." The last book of the Bible, Revelation, refers to this judgment. "If anyone's name was not found written in the book of life, that person was thrown into the lake of fire" (20:15 NET).

Animals do not have a soul, like people do, and as such have not sinned or rebelled against a holy God. People were created in a separate act of creation from the animals, setting humans apart. People were also created in God's image, but animals were not. In the first book of the Bible, we read, "Then God said, 'Let us make human beings in our image, to be like us. They will reign over the fish in the sea, the birds in the sky, the livestock, all the wild animals on the earth, and the small animals that scurry along the ground'" (Gen. 1:26 NLT). Since humans were created in God's image, they are superior to the animal kingdom and are to rule over them.

To be created in the image of God includes a moral nature in people. In other words, animals are not considered personally responsible for evil choices, but people are. If a bear kills a person, we put it to death to prevent further attacks, not because we hold it ethically responsible for murder. But moral and ethical choices like murder and adultery are charged against people since they have a moral nature and are responsible to God for their moral choices. Jesus had to die directly for all people to pay the penalty for their individual rebellion against God's holy standards. He didn't die for the "sins" of animals since they don't sin like people.

But even though animals don't sin, the entire universe became cursed at the rebellion of the first two humans, Adam and Eve. So death and decay pervade everything: the planets, the stars, and all the animals that live on earth.

The good news is that just as Jesus' death paid the penalty so that we might one day be resurrected to a new body, Jesus' death made it possible that one day the whole world might be released from its curse to become a beautiful, renewed earth. The Bible says it this way: "Against its will, all creation was subjected to God's curse. But with eager hope, the creation looks forward to the day when it will join God's children in glorious freedom from death and decay" (Rom. 8:20–21 NLT).

There is no direct statement in the Bible that declares that animals will be re-created to live in heaven. Neither are there any direct comments in the Bible that declare that God won't. But some *implications* exist that he will restore the animal kingdom in heaven. First, the passage above (Rom. 8:20–21) says that in some future day when God's children receive a "glorious freedom from death and decay," God will also bring about a freedom from death and decay for all of his creation. This "creation" includes animals. So animals without death and decay must exist on the new earth. They seem to exist in heaven now. The apostle John saw a vision of God's presence (Rev. 4:1) in which there were four living creatures, three of which had similar appearances to the lion, the ox, and the eagle (vv. 4:6–7). Later, John somehow saw or heard "every creature in heaven and on earth and under the earth and on the sea, and all that is in them" expressing praise to God (5:13).

Many Bible interpreters debate whether Isaiah 11:6 is about heaven, but even if it's not, it gives a picture that shows how God can change animals and demonstrate his love for them (and for us who love animals). "Leopards will lie down with young goats, and wolves will rest with lambs. Calves and lions will eat together and be cared for by little children" (CEV). So I think these implications suggest that animals will be in "heaven" (or better, on the new earth).

Second, wherever possible, God by his nature ultimately desires to restore rather than discard what he has created. God desires to resurrect our death-bound bodies rather than to discard them. Our future bodies will be remade into ones that will be similar to our old bodies, yet free from suffering and pain. These new bodies will function perfectly—even in supernatural ways. Don't we think it best to restore a valuable painting of a famous artist rather than just toss it out?

God thinks the same way. One day he will remake the old earth into what the Bible calls the new earth (cf. 2 Peter 3:13; Rev. 21:1). He won't just destroy the old earth (see question #10). So perhaps this hints at his delight in restoring animals to live with us on the new earth.

But even if there will be animals on the new earth, less information is given to us in the Bible about whether individual animals like our pets will be brought back to life from the dead. In other words, there are fewer inferences that suggest that our pets will be "resurrected." The Bible just doesn't speak clearly about this, and it seems somewhat unlikely, since they don't have souls like people do.

But as a pet lover, I take comfort in the fact that God is the giver of all good gifts. Jesus said, "If you, then, though you are evil, know how to give good gifts to your children, how much more will your Father in heaven give good gifts to those who ask him!" (Matt. 7:11). The new earth will be filled only with marvelous things to enjoy. I've had four dogs that I loved who have now died. Yet the three dogs I have now help me forget the pets I had years ago. I think the animals and pets we may have in heaven might replace the love we had for all our earthly pets. Maybe they will even be near replicas of our earthly pets. But they may also be even better pets than we've ever had. Imagine petting a tame lion or riding a dolphin! Billy Graham said, "God will prepare everything for our perfect happiness in heaven, and if it takes my dog being there, I believe he'll be there."

FOR FURTHER STUDY

Genesis 1:21, 25, 31; Exodus 23:12; Deuteronomy 25:4; Proverbs 12:10; Isaiah 11:1–10; Jonah 4:11

16 Does anything ever change in heaven?

I don't like change. Just ask my wife. As I was writing this book, my wife decided to change my office. She secretly bought me a used oak rolltop desk to replace my drab metal office desk. Then she decided to purchase new bookshelves to replace the older wood bookshelves she thought were ugly. It's not so much change that I dislike. It's things that are foreign or unknown to me. All my books and files were in the hallway for a few weeks. What if some files I needed were in a box at the bottom of the stack of six boxes? People like me don't like the unknown. If I travel to Timbuktu, will I be able to tolerate the food?

Some things won't change in heaven. God will never change. Neither will Jesus. The writer of the book of Hebrews claims, "Jesus Christ is the same yesterday and today and forever" (13:8). In heaven we will be sinless. That will never change. We will be eternally holy. I will never again lie, cheat, steal, lust, be greedy, have impure motives, and on and on. That's very encouraging—both to me and to *everyone* who will know me in heaven! But just because God and Jesus don't change in their nature and character, and just because our holiness will never change, doesn't mean there won't be any change at all in heaven.

With no changes at all, things get depressing really quickly. Who wants to wear the same clothing for months and years, let alone for eternity? Sometimes we need a change of scenery, a change of foods to eat, a change of colors on the wall of our living room. Like oxygen, change is a basic need of humanity. Why else is it considered a punishment to be locked in a prison cell? Ultimately, we all need and love variety.

If people will be entirely happy in heaven (and they will), it is essential that heaven be thoroughly human in its activities and conditions. That includes an assortment of activities. Imagination and curiosity are also fundamental to our being. Without future goals that involve innovation, together with rational and emotional elements, heaven would not be heaven. Humanity was created and destined for change and variety. Without variation and creativity, there is no joy and happiness.

God loves the "new." The Bible is filled with this word. Paul told the Corinthian Christians, "If anyone is in Christ, the new creation has come: The old has gone, the new is here!" (2 Cor.

5:17). In Revelation, a "new song" was sung at the throne of God (14:3). It is also recorded that God will declare at the beginning of eternity, "I am making everything new" (21:5). Heaven is all about the continuing of new things. God is a God who creates. This is who he is. He will never stop creating new things.

If the new heaven and new earth are a reflection of the old heaven and the old earth, we should expect an incredible variety in the eternal earth. What if you had a lifetime to explore this world? Each place you chose to visit and investigate would be distinct and unique. One lifetime would not be nearly enough time to exhaust the adventures of this world. But we will have an eternity to explore the new heavens and the new earth. Perhaps there will even be distant worlds or multiple universes to visit. If God will make all things new, how long will it take for us to seek out, explore, and study all these things made new? An eternity! That's variety and change.

There are approximately 10,000 different species of birds in the world, 20,000 species of butterflies, and 40,000 species of spiders. I think God knows about variety—and loves it. Heaven will involve constant variety.

FOR FURTHER STUDY

Isaiah 43:19; 48:6; Matthew 24:35; Hebrews 1:12; 7:21; 13:8; 1 John 2:17

17 Will we be bored in heaven?

Most of human culture maintains the underlying assumption that sin is fun and holiness is dull and uninteresting. If we subscribe to such an idea, we have been misled. Since God knows all things, he knows more about what is fun for us than we do ourselves. He made us. Solomon wrote about God, "Without him, who can eat or find enjoyment?" (Eccl. 2:25).

Paul claimed that the God who works in the believer's heart "is able to do immeasurably more than all we ask or imagine" (Eph. 3:20). Whatever we envision the pleasures of heaven will be, God can make them immeasurably more than our greatest imagination! "You will fill me with joy in your presence, with eternal pleasures at your right hand" (Ps. 16:11), wrote David, the great king and songwriter.

C. S. Lewis (1898–1963), author of the well-known novel *The Lion, the Witch, and the Wardrobe*, once said, "Joy is a serious business of heaven." In another book Lewis described an adult trying to explain to a child that the greatest pleasure on earth is sexual pleasure. The boy thinks that eating chocolates is the greatest pleasure. We are like the boy, unfamiliar with the pleasures of heaven. Lewis commented, "We know the sexual pleasure. We don't know, except in glimpses, the other thing, which in Heaven, will leave no room for [sexual pleasure in comparison]."

Eternal pleasures! What are the greatest earthly pleasures? Sex? Is that boring? But God created sex. It was his idea, not ours. Eating our favorite food? Is that boring? God created eating. It was his idea, not ours. All earthly pleasures involve our sight, hearing, touch, smell, and taste—the five senses. They were all invented by God. They were his creation. They all can be used righteously as well as sinfully. In heaven, we will use all our senses in godly ways in our resurrected bodies. God may even create additional sensory experiences unknown to us on earth. Perhaps we will be able to hear all the pitches that a dog can hear. Our eyes may be able to distinguish more colors, or see at a greater distance. Our tongue may savor astounding flavors now unknown to people.

Mark Twain claimed there would be no humor in heaven. I disagree. Think for a moment of all the strange and funny animals God created such as the ostrich, penguin, giraffe, clown fish, anteater, aardvark, baboon, and more. God made them all. God is the creator of all things, even humor. A careful reading of the Bible uncovers some very humorous comments, mostly on the subtle side. Just a few days after Jesus' death and resurrection, he appeared to two men on a road leading away from Jerusalem. The two men didn't recognize Jesus at first. As he conversed with them, one of them asked, "Are you the only one visiting Jerusalem who does not know the things that have happened there in these days?" (Luke 24:18). They were *so* wrong!

Much of the humor in the Bible is irony. Peter, the well-known apostle of Christ, was given the nickname "Rock" (think "rocky"). But his personality was impetuous, and he tended to say foolish things. Peter told Jesus, "I will lay down my life for you" (John 13:37). Then a few hours later he denied he knew Jesus three times. While cross-examining Jesus, Pilate asked, "What is truth?" (18:38). But Truth was standing right in front of him!

The Old Testament prophet Elijah challenged the prophets of the pagan god Baal to a test. Elijah and the prophets of Baal would each prepare a sacrifice to their god and pray. The god that answered their prayers by lighting a fire from heaven under their sacrifice would be the true god. The prophets of Baal prayed first. When no fire appeared under the sacrifice to Baal, "Elijah began making fun of them. 'Pray louder!' he said. 'Baal must be a god. Maybe he's day-dreaming or using the toilet or traveling somewhere. Or maybe he's asleep, and you have to wake him up'" (1 Kings 18:27 CEV).

In the Bible we find no record of angels in heaven being bored. God is the author of everything that is fascinating. For one thing, angels are fascinated by all the different aspects of God's wisdom. "Through the church the complicated, many-sided wisdom of God in all its infinite variety and innumerable aspects might now be made known to the angelic rulers . . ." (Eph. 3:10 AMP). For all eternity, we too will see more and more of God's manifold wisdom in sacrificing his Son on the cross for our forgiveness.

Boredom arises from waiting. But there will be no waiting for something better in heaven. Every moment will be the best ever. Make no mistake about it! There will be no dull days in heaven.

But if there were, a "dull" day in heaven would be more exciting than the most thrilling day we have ever had on earth.

FOR FURTHER STUDY

Psalm 31:19; 84:11; Romans 8:28; 1 Corinthians 2:9; 2 Corinthians 12:3–4; 1 Peter 1:12

18 Will we know our Christian friends and loved ones in heaven?

Some of us are old enough to look back on our high school pictures and chuckle at how we looked. We laugh at these early pictures because we see the outdated styles of hair and clothes. Pictures from elementary school are even more hilarious as we see chubby cheeks, Coke-bottle glasses, and funny clothes. Most often we can recognize resemblances between the person now and how they looked many years earlier. Over the years I have had a mustache, partial beard, or full beard. Anyone who has known me well when I was clean shaven could still recognize me now that I have a beard.

When we get to heaven, our recognition of friends and family will be much like being able to recognize a friend's photo from the past. Many features of our friends and relatives will have dramatically changed from the time of life on earth, but many other features will be retained and will be identifying characteristics distinct to who they are. Those to whom Jesus appeared after his resurrection recognized him as the same Jewish rabbi and teacher he was on earth. His identity didn't change. Neither will ours.

While we will have youthful bodies in heaven with no signs of aging, we will maintain our unique identity, including race and gender. "Abraham breathed his last and died . . . and he was gathered to his people" (Gen. 25:8). "Gathered to his people" means that in death Abraham joined others of his race in the present heaven, including his wife, Sarah, who had died earlier. Abraham was Jewish on earth; he will be so in heaven. If we were African American on earth, we will be African American in heaven. Race is part of our identity. Racial profiling and gender discrimination will be unknown in heaven. There will be Chinese, Germans, Americans, Koreans, Arabs—many from all different racial groups.

Personality is also a part of our identity. God has made a variety of personalities, with no one personality type being his ideal. We will be able to recognize our friends and family members by their personality. Our personalities will be the same in heaven, but with all sinful tendencies removed.

A fascinating account is given about the physical reappearance of two leaders of the Old Testament, Moses and Elijah, to three of Jesus' disciples (Matt. 17:1–8). The three disciples recognized Moses, dead for over fourteen hundred years, and Elijah, taken up to heaven by God over eight hundred years before. Despite these facts, Peter, James, and John had no trouble instantly identifying them. How did they do this? Simply, it was a miracle. Heaven will be just as miraculous. We will recognize those of our friends and family who have also come to heaven by faith in Christ even though they will look youthful.

Like the three disciples who immediately knew Moses and Elijah without ever having known them personally, we too will instantly identify Peter, James, and John without ever having met them. Our names are also part of our identity that will not change. We will know them by name and they will immediately know us by name.

Perhaps this is why Paul wrote, "All that I know now is partial and incomplete, but then I will know everything completely, just as God now knows me completely" (1 Cor. 13:12 NLT). Only

God is omniscient. Our knowledge will not be as exhaustive as his is. Nevertheless, our knowledge may include an instantaneous recognition of the identity of every person we meet in heaven, including their names. Imagine meeting and conversing with important characters of the Bible, or great men and women of faith throughout history.

My two sons on earth are adult Christian believers. When they were preteens and teens, I related to them as my sons in a way that was appropriate for their age. When they became adults, changes took place in how we carried out the father-son relationship. Someday we will be in heaven together. I delight in that comforting thought. They will still be my sons in heaven, but we will relate to each other in a different way than we did on earth. Our relationship will be even deeper then, for we will be transformed into perfect people.

Paul comforted the believers of Thessalonica by explaining that their Christian friends who had died would be reunited with them one day in heaven (1 Thess. 4:13–18). What comfort is this for the Thessalonians if they were not able to recognize their friends in heaven? Of course, they will.

FOR FURTHER STUDY

Genesis 35:29; 49:33; 2 Samuel 12:23; Luke 24:31; John 20:11–16; Revelation 21:12–14

19 Are there marriages and families in heaven?

For many people, the closest relationships they have on earth are their family relationships. Their closest friend is a brother or sister, a husband or wife, or perhaps even a father or mother. God himself created the idea of families and their innate bonding powers. The father-son relationship on earth is patterned after God the Father and his Son. When a family is a family of believing Christians, it is natural to long for a reunion of that family in heaven. My father and mother were both followers of Jesus. They are both now in heaven. I will rejoice to see them someday. Will I know them in heaven as my parents? Yes. But how we relate to one another in heaven will change.

On one occasion, Jesus was questioned by the Sadducees. This Jewish religious group did not believe in a future resurrection as did Jesus (and the majority of the Jews in Israel). They attempted to trick Jesus with a hypothetical question about a woman who had a husband who died. After she remarried, her second husband died. This happened with seven husbands. Then the woman also died. "Whose wife will she be in the resurrection?" they asked. The Sadducees thought they had won the argument. Jesus replied, "At the resurrection people will neither marry nor be given in marriage; they will be like the angels in heaven" (Matt. 22:30).

Married couples will remember and celebrate in heaven the relationship they had on earth (if it was a loving and harmonious relationship). But their relationship in heaven will change. How will their relationship change? All believers will become our closest friends and companions, just like our wife or husband was on earth.

Once, "Jesus' mother and brothers came to see him, but they were not able to get near him because of the crowd." Jesus used the circumstances to teach spiritual truth. "My mother and brothers are those who hear God's word and put it into practice" (Luke 8:19–21). Ultimately, we do not lose an earthly relationship; we gain multiple heavenly relationships. There will be just one big family in heaven.

Some lament the fact that there is no marriage in heaven. Others are disillusioned that there must be no sex in heaven either. God actually created the sexual relationship between a man and a woman to be a picture of the intimacy that people can have spiritually with Christ. Paul wrote, "A man will leave his father and mother and be united to his wife, and the two will become one flesh. This is a profound mystery. . . ." By "become one flesh," the apostle was speaking of the sexual relationship in marriage. Then he added, "But I am talking about Christ and the church" (Eph. 5:31–32). In other words, sexual pleasure was designed to capture the intensity of the believer's joy in a relationship with Jesus. In the Bible, Jesus is called the bridegroom and his followers are called the bride. So the sexual relationship on earth foreshadows the relationship Christian believers will have with Christ in heaven. No one in heaven will ever miss earthly marriage, for we will all be married to the Lord.

The best marriages on earth are the ones in which both spouses are progressing in their relationship with Christ on earth. The closer they move toward God, the closer they move toward one another. This closeness to Jesus will just continue in heaven and become deeper. Why wouldn't a married couple's relationship continue to become deeper and deeper as well?

Will there be sexual expression in heaven? The Bible doesn't speak to this directly. Sex was created by God before sin came into the human race. So sexual expression would not be excluded from heaven because it was evil. In heaven there will be sexual distinction. Those who were female on earth will be female in heaven. The same will be true for males. Jesus was a man and is a man for all eternity in his resurrected body.

God's creation of sex was for pleasure, but it was also for procreation. In heaven, there will be no bearing of children, no reproduction. It seems likely that this pleasure will be taken away and replaced with other, new desires, perhaps unknown and unrevealed to us yet. We can be sure of this: Whenever God replaces something in heaven with what we have had on earth, it is always a major upgrade. It will always be something far better!

FOR FURTHER STUDY

Matthew 22:23–32; Mark 10:29–30; Ephesians 3:14–15; Revelation 19:7–9; 21:9

20 Will we remember our earthly life in heaven?

The older people get, the more forgetful they become. That's a fact of life. It can be depressing when we begin to lose our memory. My wife and I humorously remind each other that as we get older we can watch our favorite movies over and over again as if seeing them for the first time. We have forgotten all the plots and dialogue since we watched them last.

What about in heaven? Will our memories of earth, especially bad ones, be wiped from our consciousness? We all have memories that are painful to recall. Perhaps it is a loss of a loved one that brings back deep sorrow, even after many years have gone by. Or it could be a memory of an embarrassing situation that haunts us every time we are reminded of it. Then there are sins that we have committed that we completely regret. Will these be in our memory for eternity?

In the Old Testament, King David of Israel secretly committed adultery with Bathsheba, the wife of a man named Uriah, a soldier in David's army. Bathsheba became pregnant, so David made arrangements for Uriah to be placed in the very front lines of battle, and he was killed. Then David took Bathsheba as his wife, and the pregnancy was thought to be the outcome of their new marriage. But David's murder and adultery were exposed by a prophet of God. Later the story was recorded in Scripture for millions of people to read, even to this day.

Will God in eternity do away with some of the stories of Scripture? Isaiah claimed, "The grass withers and the flowers fall, but the word of our God endures forever" (Isa. 40:8). We will always know about David's sin, and he himself will always remember that he acted wickedly. But these sins will be remembered in light of the grace God gave David in forgiving him. How will we fully be able to appreciate Jesus' suffering and death on the cross for us unless we remember our sins?

Will the apostle Paul remember who he was as a nonbelieving Jewish man? Or will his memory be wiped clear of the fact that he himself said he "was once a blasphemer and a persecutor and a violent man" (1 Tim. 1:13)? How will we understand who Paul is in heaven if we can't associate him with his persecution of the early Christian church before he came to faith? This is part of his identity. How could we remember this in heaven, but not Paul? Will we not remember that Peter denied Jesus three times on earth? Could we remember this but not Peter? Will this incident be expunged from the memory of the other disciples? All this seems unlikely.

It seems clear that not all memories, if any, are erased in heaven. It is more likely that God will heal all our memories by expanding our knowledge, rather than decreasing our memory. Because of our sin on earth, we have learned many valuable life lessons while alive. These important lessons will not vanish or be lost but will be expanded in eternity.

In heaven, God may give us unforeseeable explanations for our sorrows that we could never have seen on earth. Look at the underside of a skillfully woven quilt. The patchwork seems shabby and the stitching is odd. There is no clear image or attractive design.

But on the topside, the quilt is absolutely beautiful with matchless artistry. God in heaven is weaving a quilt. We are on the underside. Not all of life makes sense. But one day we will be on the heaven side of the quilt, viewing the sovereign but marvelous handiwork of God. We will be satisfied with both the love and justice of God.

John pictured a group in heaven who will be martyred on earth. He pictured how God "will wipe away every tear from their eyes" (Rev. 7:17). Be assured of this. In eternity, all sorrow will be gone. All righteous desire for revenge will be satisfied. All conviction, all regrets, and all embarrassment for our own sins will be taken away. There will be only thanksgiving for Jesus' cleansing of our guilt. Nothing will rob us of the most stupendous joy the earth has ever known.

FOR FURTHER STUDY

Isaiah 43:18; 65:16–18; Jeremiah 31:34; Luke 16:25; Hebrews 10:17; 1 Peter 1:25; Revelation 21:4

21 Is heaven a physical place?

Many different religions and philosophies consider anything that is physical to be corrupt or evil, and anything that is immaterial to be spiritual and good. Ancient Greek philosophy like that taught by Plato (ca. 429–347 BC) promoted this ideology. Many Eastern religions such as Hinduism believe that the body is an evil to be suppressed and that the spirit must escape this physical prison. Throughout the history of the Western world, various offshoots of Christianity have also mistakenly taught that the material/physical world is sinful. This is not what the Bible teaches.

Angels are nonmaterial and are holy. Demons are also nonmaterial beings. Yet demons are evil even though they are spirit/spiritual. The physical universe was created by God. Before sin entered the world, the creation was fully approved by God. He saw that it was good, mentioned seven times in Genesis 1. God commanded Adam and Eve to be fruitful and multiply. In order to obey this divine command, the first couple had to have sexual relations, a physical act. Sex was a holy experience in this first marital union. It is not the use but the misuse of physical things that corrupts. Physical things like money and possessions are made gods that replace the one true God. Jesus taught that it is the heart and mind that defile a person—not outward, physical things.

Since there will be continuity between the old earth and the new earth, the new earth must be physical like the old earth. The new Jerusalem, the central city on the new earth, must have some evident continuity with the natural city of Jerusalem on earth. It too must be physical (see question #22). What meaning would a nonphysical "city" have on a physical earth, or a physical city have on a "spiritual," immaterial earth?

Jesus will be on the new earth with a physical body, the same body people touched after his resurrection on earth. All true believers will be in physical bodies on the new earth as well. The physical resurrection of the bodies of all Christian believers makes no sense unless there is a corresponding physical new earth in which we will live.

Jesus told his disciples the night before his death, "My Father's house has many rooms; if that were not so, would I have told you that I am going there to prepare a place for you? And if I go and prepare a place for you, I will come back and take you to be with me that you also may be where I am" (John 14:2–3). A "place," "rooms," and "house" all have physical properties. Clearly, the new earth will have physical properties.

What about the temporary heaven? Is it physical? We know that Jesus is in heaven right now, and he is there in a physical body. The book of Hebrews tells us that after his ascension into heaven, Jesus "sat down at the right hand of the throne of God" (12:2). Is Jesus' physical body resting on an immaterial, ethereal throne in heaven? This doesn't seem likely. When Stephen was being stoned to death, he saw a heavenly vision of "the Son of Man standing at the right hand of God" (Acts 7:56). What was Jesus' physical body standing on? Was he suspended in midair? Not likely.

Men and women of faith in the Old Testament came to the land of Israel from other countries. "They [were] looking for a country of their own. If they had been thinking of the country they had left, they would have had opportunity to return. Instead, they were longing for a better country—a heavenly one. Therefore God is not ashamed to be called their God, for he has prepared a city for them" (Heb. 11:14–16). A "heavenly country" doesn't mean nonphysical. A "better country" implies some physical continuity with an earthly, physical "country" that was not as good. God has prepared a city. All this sounds very physical.

In another place, the unknown author of Hebrews encouraged his readers: "You suffered along with those in prison and joyfully accepted the confiscation of your property, because you knew that you yourselves had better and lasting possessions" (10:34). Aren't "possessions" something physical? I think so.

FOR FURTHER STUDY

Mark 7:18–23; 1 Timothy 6:17; Hebrews 1:3; 10:12; 11:26; 1 Peter 1:4; Revelation 4:1–11

22 What is the new Jerusalem?

I'm a country person at heart. Cities don't get me excited. But others love the cities, teeming with people and activities. If you are looking for sports events, great restaurants, operas, museums, etc., you will find them in the city.

The new earth will have a new city called the new Jerusalem. The name "Jerusalem" recalls the ancient city of the Old Testament and the Jewish temple there. The temple was where God promised to meet personally with his people. So first and foremost, the new Jerusalem will be where God lives in community with his people.

Old Testament men and women of faith were "longing for a better country—a heavenly one" (Heb. 11:16). By faith, Abraham "made his home in the promised land like a stranger in a foreign country," but he lived in tents as a nomad. By faith "he was looking forward to the city [i.e., the new Jerusalem] with foundations, whose architect and builder is God" (v. 10). Tents have no foundations, but the new Jerusalem certainly will.

The new Jerusalem is already in existence in heaven. When eternity begins, the new Jerusalem will come down out of heaven to be permanently joined to the new earth as the center of all activity. A city means community, and the new Jerusalem will be a place of ongoing love, friendship, and cooperation. All earthly cities or communities fail to really provide perfect love and friendship.

The first wedding I ever performed was quite ordinary—except for the location. It was on the Mount of Olives, overlooking the modern city of Jerusalem. But like with every wedding, the bride was the center of attention. I've never seen a bride who wasn't beautifully dressed. John wrote, "I saw the Holy City, the new Jerusalem, coming down out of heaven from God, prepared as a bride beautifully dressed for her husband" (Rev. 21:2).

The apostle employs the same imagery of a bride to describe how marvelous the new Jerusalem will be. It will be an amazingly beautiful city! No smog, chaotic traffic, crowded sidewalks, or the like. This city will be perfectly matched to our needs and will be as attractive to us as a bride is to her husband. It also will be the only "Holy City" that has ever existed. No crime, violence, gangs, murder, theft, political corruption, or anything like it will be in this city. The fact that it is called "the new Jerusalem" will always remind us of the old Jerusalem where the Savior, the Lord Jesus, died and rose again to bring us everlasting life.

Just as precious jewels add beauty to any woman, especially a bride, the new Jerusalem is adorned with a wide variety of enormous brilliant, priceless gems. Twelve foundation stones, each with a distinct rare gem and dominant color, provide permanence to the city (vv. 19–20). The city itself is made of pure gold, with what looked to John to be a radiant "transparent glass" (v. 21).

There are also twelve gates to the city, and each is made from an immense single pearl (v. 21). These gate-towers are carefully guarded by twelve sentinel angels, one at each gate (v. 12). Despite all the jokes about St. Peter at the Pearly Gates, in the Bible the famous apostle never has this responsibility.

Nothing unholy and no one impure will break through to God's presence. The walls of the city are 144 cubits or 216 feet wide (v. 17). Ancient Near-Eastern cities had thick walls for protection. The new Jerusalem will have complete security and free access, in and out, for all its inhabitants.

Surely descriptions like these are designed to accommodate our finite understanding. Imagine someone from the first century being transported into a vision of the twenty-first century with its cars, planes, cell phones, tablets, and laptops. How would that ancient visitor describe the phenomena around him? So also, how else could John describe the vision he had of the unfathomable glory of God and the eternal dwelling God will create for us!

The inhabitants of the new Jerusalem will be all those who had faith in the one true God of Israel (the Old Testament believers) or who placed their faith in Jesus (New Testament believers). This is pictured in the fact that the new Jerusalem has twelve gates (three on each side of the city) on which are written the names of the twelve tribes of Israel (vv. 12–13), which visualizes Old Testament believers by citing the leaders of each tribe. The city also has twelve foundation stones on which are written the names of the twelve New Testament apostles (v. 14), visualizing New Testament believers as well by listing the names of the leaders of the church.

The surprising thing about the new Jerusalem is that we don't go up to live with God; he comes down to live with us on the new earth. The apostle John wrote, "I heard a loud shout from the throne, saying, 'Look, God's home is now among his people! He will live with them. . . . God himself will be with them'" (21:3 NLT). Keep in mind that "his people" will include some from "every tribe and language and people and nation" (5:9).

The book of Revelation describes the new Jerusalem as shaped like a cube, about 1,400 miles (2,200 kilometers) in each direction (21:16). Bible scholars have debated whether this is literal, with symbolic meaning, or just symbolic. Either way, it communicates wonderful insights about our future home. The cube shape, with every side equal in length, suggests universal equality for all people. If the dimensions are literal, we will probably be capable of traveling vertically just as easily as we move horizontally on this earth. The length and width of this enormous city is half the size of the United States.

The Most Holy Place, the inner room of the temple in the Old Testament, was also cube shaped. Although John saw no temple in the new Jerusalem (v. 22), it is likely that the future city itself will be the "temple," the place where we will fellowship with God and with the Lamb forever. (The lamb was the primary sacrificial animal in the Old Testament used to picture the sacrifice of the Messiah for our sins. So the "Lamb" in the book of Revelation is Jesus.)

If the city were divided into vertical levels ("floors"?) 20 feet high, there would be 264 levels for each mile, and 369,600 levels, or total "floors," each having 1,400 square miles horizontally. If everyone received an acre plot ("condos"?) on the first level, there would be 869,000 acre plots on just that level alone. Regardless of how the city is structured, there will be *plenty* of room for *plenty* of people in the new Jerusalem.

No prejudice between the sexes or the races will exist in this city. Like the universal directions of north, south, east, and west, the new Jerusalem will have three gates on each of its four sides, portraying God's worldwide outreach. Anyone who believes in Jesus regardless of language, nationality, race, or origin can become a resident in this city.

Several things are absent from the new Jerusalem besides the temple. The earthly temple always involved limited access to God through various holy rooms and the specially selected priests. In the new Jerusalem, we will have unrestricted access to God and the Lamb. There will be no need for the sun or the moon either, since God himself will be the light (Rev. 21:23). Nor will there be anything impure, unclean, immoral, or deceitful that will enter the city, and there won't be any people who do these things either.

Finally, a river that contains "the water of life" flows from the very throne of God and of the Lamb (22:1). The water of life represents the free gift of eternal life offered to all who respond in faith to Jesus (John 4:10–14). Eternal life comes to us without any cost to ourselves (Rev. 21:6; 22:17). The Tree of Life, which bears twelve crops of fruit every month, is also in the city. The Tree of Life recalls the idyllic garden of Eden before the curse on the earth (Gen. 2:9; 3:22, 24). In the new Jerusalem, there will be no more curse (Rev. 22:3).

FOR FURTHER STUDY

Isaiah 26:1; Galatians 4:26; Ephesians 2:20; Revelation 21:1–27; 22:1–5

23 Will we be singing and playing harps all the time in heaven?

There are very few people who don't like music. It is estimated that the music industry makes over $60 billion each year. God is the one who created the idea of music both for our enjoyment and our praise of his marvels. Our vocal cords are fashioned so that music (of greater or lesser skill) can be easily produced. The book of Psalms in the Old Testament contains 150 individual poems, most or all of which were sung by the Jewish people in the temple or at other celebrations. Jesus himself sang with his disciples at his last Passover meal before his crucifixion (Mark 14:26).

Music is composed of only eight notes but is arranged in variations of sharps and flats with unlimited octaves, innumerable rhythms, and perhaps eternal possibilities of melody and harmony. Different cultures create different styles of music on different instruments that are seemingly endless in potential. This may be so since God himself, the creator of music, is endless and eternal.

There will be more instruments in heaven than harps. In the worship of the Lord on earth, the Bible also mentions various trumpets, animal horns (e.g., ram's horn), bells, flutes, cymbals, tambourines, lyres, drums, string instruments, reed instruments, and more. Will the intermediate heaven or the new earth have fewer instruments than the present earth? Unlikely. But it is not clear in the Bible that every person in heaven will play an instrument in worship.

Will our activities in heaven be restricted to a formal worship of God? If you never knew another Christian, but one day someone took you to a Sunday church service in which there was much singing, would you conclude that Christians sing and worship all the time and do nothing else? Probably not! And just because there are several scenes in the Bible where angels or Christians sing and worship in heaven doesn't mean that is what we will do all the time there.

Most people don't go through a day without hearing some music somewhere, somehow—on a CD, radio, iPod, smartphone, TV, podcast, Internet, or some other way. But most people, even music lovers, don't listen to music all the time. There are other activities they need to do.

There will be regular times of singing and music in heaven. But the variety of songs sung in honor of God will be phenomenal. We don't get wearied with all our music on earth because new songs are continually being generated. We even have radically different styles, from country to gospel, from opera to rap.

The book of Revelation has the most references of any Bible book to songs being sung in heaven. Several times it mentions heavenly characters singing a "new song" (5:9; 14:3). In Revelation 15:3, a group of faithful Christians sing "the song of God's servant Moses and of the Lamb." They have creatively updated Moses' Old Testament song in light of the work of Jesus, the revealed Messiah. Six times the book of Psalms mentions singing a "new song." So the creation of new songs in heaven will be God's delight for his servants. Perhaps songs written on earth that honor and praise Jesus will be updated for singing in heaven.

The activities of heaven will be greatly varied. Besides singing and worshiping, we will be governing, serving, creating, building, writing, learning, teaching, painting, drawing, designing, composing, reading, laughing, playing, traveling, exploring, eating, drinking, socializing, conversing... the list is as endless as the heaven in which we will live. We must never suppose that our earthly life will have *anything* in it more pleasing or more enjoyable than our heavenly life. Earth is the closest that a non-Christian will ever get to heaven. Earth is the closest a believing Christian will ever get to hell.

FOR FURTHER STUDY
Psalm 33:3; Jeremiah 29:11; Matthew 22:1–2; Revelation 7:15; 22:5

24 Will there be time in eternity?

Time seems to be a negative part of our lives. If it wasn't for time, I could read all the books I wanted. But I am a very slow reader, and time is short in this life. I have to carefully select which books are the most important, and leave many other good books unread. Yet time is not the problem. Sin brought death and a curse on humanity. Death restricts our time on earth, and aging frustrates our lives with its limits. Science fiction writers have solved the problem through time travel. In 1895, H. G. Wells wrote the novel *Time Machine*, which has been adapted into two major movies. Still, only God can travel through time because he alone is timeless and omnipresent.

The book of Revelation was written to the seven churches in the province of Asia (Turkey). The book opens with the greeting, "Grace and peace to you from him who is, and who was, and who is to come . . ." (1:4). John was referring to God, the one who exists in the past, present, and future. There was never a "time" when God didn't exist, because he was never created. But people can't escape time. Before the creation of the world, there was no time. Time and space (creation) go together. Time is part of the very nature of creation and humanity.

Traditionally, Christians have thought that eternity will be timeless. Some have based this on the reading of Revelation 10:6 in the King James Version, "there should be time no longer." But modern versions show the true intent of the statement, and translate, "There will be no more delay!" or "The time is up" (CEB).

The Bible suggests that people in the present or intermediate heaven are fully conscious of time. In John's supernatural vision of martyred Christians now in heaven, he heard them say, " 'Lord, the One who is holy and true, how long until You judge and avenge our blood from those who live on the earth?' So a white robe was given to each of them, and they were told to rest a little while longer. . . ." (6:10–11 HCSB).

Why would these martyrs cry out, "How long?" unless in their heavenly lives they were conscious of time? Why would the Lord reply to them, "Rest a little while longer," if time in heaven were no more? Even the conversation between the martyrs and the Lord

72

implies time. The martyrs spoke first, and then the Lord gave his reply. This is a sequence of events. Wherever there is a sequence of events, there is time.

There is singing in heaven. Twenty-four elders in heaven worship Jesus, the Lamb, with singing (5:8–10). Music implies time. One note follows another, and one stanza follows another. We can speak of a previous note and a future note to the one we just sang.

Earthly time may be similar to heavenly time. After a series of divine judgments on earth, Revelation states that "there was silence in heaven for about half an hour" (8:1). Even in the eternal state and on the new earth, there seems to be a calendar. John described what he saw in the new Jerusalem: "On each side of the river [of life] stood the tree of life, bearing twelve crops of fruit, yielding its fruit every month" (22:2). The implication is that there is a cycle of twelve months on the new earth just like we have twelve months in a year on earth.

In J. R. R. Tolkien's *The Fellowship of the Ring*, Bilbo Baggins ponders how wonderful the Elf paradise of Rivendell is. "Time doesn't seem to pass here. It just is." Since there is endless time in heaven, we will always reach fulfillment and satisfaction, yet always be progressing. If we can learn more about God and grow closer to him, then there is time in heaven. But the good news of time in heaven is that we will never be in a hurry, never fear being late or missing an appointment, never be pressured by a deadline. We will never be restless or idle, never bored or irritated, and never have to look at a watch or clock. There will be no delays or waiting in lines. And no one will grow older!

FOR FURTHER STUDY

Genesis 8:22; Isaiah 60:22–23; Ephesians 2:7; 2 Peter 3:8; Revelation 7:15

25 Will we see God in heaven?

It's humorous to look back on an era without cell phones. When my wife and I watch an old TV program or movie, we often laugh at the ring of an old desk phone or the telephone booth some movie star had to use while away from home. Today, we expect to see on our cell phone, computer, or tablet the face of the person we want to talk to. Why do we want to see their face? Because it is much more personal than just a voice. Face-to-face communication is a step up from communicating merely by voice.

Face-to-face communication with God is not something to be taken for granted. In the garden of Eden before the sin of Adam and Eve, God lived and walked with the first couple in personal friendship. They apparently were able to see God and he was obviously able to see them. But they hid themselves from him after they sinned (Gen. 3:8). From that point on in human history, people were not allowed to approach God to see him because of the sin problem, except in selective prophetic visions.

Even Moses (ca. 1450 BC) was not permitted to see God. Not long after the giving of the Ten Commandments, Moses asked God to show him his glory. God replied, "You cannot see my face, for no one may see me and live" (Ex. 33:20). God's face (his brilliant glory) would have killed Moses if he had seen God directly.

The apostle John introduced the ministry of Jesus by stating, "No one has ever seen God, but the one and only Son, who is himself God and is in closest relationship with the Father, has made him known" (John 1:18). People were able to see God indirectly by seeing Jesus, who had taken on a human (visible) body through birth. In this way, people could see God in Jesus and not die. So Jesus revealed God and his glory to people. John wrote, "The Word [Jesus] became flesh and made his dwelling among us. We have seen his glory, the glory of the one and only Son, who came from the Father, full of grace and truth" (v. 14).

In the new Jerusalem of eternity, the privilege of all those who have obeyed Jesus by placing their faith in him will be able to see God personally. Revelation 22:3–4 prophesies, "No longer will there be any curse. The throne of God and of the Lamb will be in the city, and his servants will serve him. They will see his face, and his name will be on their foreheads." To see God's face and to have his name on their foreheads pictures God's identification and personal companionship with every believer. In heaven there will be no barriers or restrictions between God and his people.

A close relationship with a spouse, family member, or friend involves having a knowledge that is held in common and mutually enjoyed. Paul seems to refer to this in his famous chapter on love: "For now we see only a reflection as in a mirror; then we shall see face to face. Now I know in part; then I shall know fully, even as I am fully known" (1 Cor. 13:12). To see God face-to-face will mean a deeper, fuller, more personal knowledge of God that cannot be attained on earth.

In the Old Testament, criminals were often banished from the presence of the king and not allowed to look upon his face again (cf. 2 Sam. 14:24; Est. 7:8). Jesus, in his famous Sermon on the Mount, explained, "Blessed are the pure in heart, for they will see God" (Matt. 5:8). Those who through faith are purified by being given the righteousness of God (see question #2) will live forever in God's presence, face-to-face.

What will be our reaction when we see God? We will be astounded by his absolute beauty. With this beauty we will experience warmth, comfort, love, peace, and complete satisfaction. David wrote, "One thing I ask from the LORD, this only do I seek: that I may dwell in the house of the LORD all the days of my life, to gaze on the beauty of the LORD . . ." (Ps. 27:4). As I mentioned before, David wasn't asking to live in an earthly temple all his life. He was longing for the eternal temple, the very presence of God.

The beauty of the Lord describes more than a literal, aesthetic experience of God. It is also the spiritual response to who God is in all of his attributes and qualities. We will perceive all at once that God has/is unattainable knowledge, unimaginable power and creativity, and unfathomable grace and love.

FOR FURTHER STUDY

Job 19:26–27; Psalm 11:7; 17:15; Daniel 7:9–14; John 14:6–10; Hebrews 12:14; 1 John 3:2; 4:12

26 What will it be like to worship God in heaven?

A number of years ago I attended a men's conference of several thousands. We met in a large football stadium in a major city in the States. With energy and power, we sang numerous Christian songs. The noise seemed to be powerful enough to collapse the walls. Then when we stopped singing to pray, there was a silence that cut through the stadium like a powerful quiet that follows a storm. The feeling of that moment was indescribable. Lightning could have come down from heaven and we wouldn't have noticed it. Perhaps it was a foretaste of heavenly worship.

Like on earth, in heaven there will be prescribed times to worship God. As we saw earlier, a picture is given in Revelation 5 of a corporate gathering for worship. At least one hundred million angels encircle God's throne in the present heaven. They are joined by four unique heavenly creatures and twenty-four "elders" who symbolically represent faithful believers. They praise both God and the Lamb (Jesus), shouting with loud voices, "To him who sits on the throne and to the Lamb be praise and honor and glory and power, for ever and ever!" (v. 13). In this heavenly scene, there is no monastic isolation or worship in silence.

But there will be plenty of informal times to worship God too. This must be done on earth. So we should expect it will be done in heaven as well. David testified, "I will extol the LORD at all times; his praise will always be on my lips" (Ps. 34:1). When I narrowly escape a car accident, I praise God for his protection and sovereignty. When I see a marvelous arboretum of trees, plants, and flowers, my instinctive response is to marvel at God's handiwork. In a similar way, much of our heavenly worship will be spontaneous and free, not restrictive or commanded. Natural, not contrived or forced. No mixed motives, no distractions, no lack of concentration.

Worship in heaven would be radically incomplete if continual praise of God failed to include thankfulness for God's plan of forgiveness for our sins. This plan was made possible through the death of Jesus. This is a reoccurring theme in John's descriptions of worship in heaven. In Revelation 5:9, a group sings praise to Jesus, "You are worthy . . . because you were slain, and with your blood you purchased for God persons from every tribe and language and people and nation." Unlike many worship gatherings on earth, this chorus is made up of people from all cultures, nations, languages, and centuries.

I once met a man who attended a church that had gone through some major remodeling. In the process, those in authority switched the location of the piano and the organ at the front of the church. The result was a major split in the congregation, many of whom were disgruntled by the new arrangement. Since there will be no sin in heaven, such selfish quarrels will be totally absent in the worship of eternity.

Worship in heaven also includes praise for God's holiness. In heaven, shouts of praise to God as envisioned in Revelation repeatedly call out his purity. "Holy, holy, holy" is shouted to God in the heavenly scenes of both Isaiah 6:3 and Revelation 4:8. In the Bible, no other quality or attribute of God is repeated this way in a triad fashion, even God's love.

Paul wrote to the believers in Rome, "I urge you, brothers and sisters, in view of God's mercy, to offer your bodies as a living sacrifice, holy and pleasing to God—this is your true and proper worship" (Rom. 12:1). What we do with our bodies is central to worship, both now and in eternity. I can praise God in a worship service on Sunday. But I can also worship God in jogging, washing the dishes, texting on my phone, or brushing my teeth. How and why we do these things shows whether or not we are worshiping God.

The same will be true in heaven. We will serve God in our resurrected bodies. *Every* activity we do in our sinless bodies on the new earth will be a holy worship of God. We will paint, teach, research, travel, act as ambassadors, build, administer God's creation, and create computer code. Eternity will involve many varied activities with which we will use our resurrected bodies. We will be wholeheartedly serving our God. This is true worship.

FOR FURTHER STUDY

Psalm 95:6; Matthew 2:1–11; John 4:23–24; Ephesians 5:19–20; Hebrews 12:22–23; Revelation 7:9–12; 19:5–6

27 Will we have bodies in heaven?

S imeon Stylites (Stylites is from the Greek word *stylos*, meaning "pillar") was a fifth-century Christian (ca. 390–459) who practiced severe treatment of the body. Although it is hard to imagine, he lived for thirty-seven years on a small platform on top of a pole near Aleppo, Syria, in an attempt to secure a place in heaven. Over the years, the height of the poles increased from thirteen feet to about fifty feet. The platform on which he lived was only about three feet square. Several other Christian ascetics followed his example.

Such severe mistreatment of the body finds no real support in the Bible, especially if one uses them in an attempt to get to heaven or be holy. Listen to what Paul said about asceticism.

> Why, as though you still belonged to the world, do you submit to its rules: "Do not handle! Do not taste! Do not touch!"? These rules . . . are based on merely human commands and teachings. Such regulations indeed have an appearance of wisdom, with their self-imposed worship, their false humility and their harsh treatment of the body, but they lack any value in restraining sensual indulgence. (Col. 2:20–23)

The basic problem with people is not the human body itself but the sinful desires inside us that control our body. While every true believer will go into the presence of Christ and God at the moment of death, all of us still await the resurrection, when we will receive an amazing resurrected body incapable of death or decay. The resurrection of our bodies will take place when Jesus returns for his followers (1 Thess. 4:16–17).

What kind of body will it be? Jesus himself had a fully human, physical body. And after his resurrection, his body was still a human, physical body subject to being seen (John 20:25) and touched (v. 27). He could walk (Luke 24:15) and eat (vv. 40–44). He also told the disciples, "Touch me and see; a ghost does not have flesh and bones, as you see I have" (v. 39). Flesh and bones. That's a physical body. But we would never say that Jesus' resurrected body was not spiritual.

There is considerable continuity between Jesus' nonresurrected and resurrected body. A few early witnesses to his resurrection did not recognize him at first. But after a brief time, all his followers who confirmed that he had truly been raised from the dead recognized him as the Jesus they knew formerly.

Paul wrote that Jesus "will take our weak mortal bodies and change them into glorious bodies like his own" (Phil. 3:21 NLT).

Jesus' resurrection is the master design for our resurrection. We will have physical bodies because he has a physical body. Somehow we think heaven will be nonphysical because something physical cannot also be spiritual. But this is not what the Bible says. "Spiritual" is not opposed to what is physical.

Paul does call our future, resurrected body a "spiritual body": "Our bodies . . . are buried in weakness, but they will be raised in strength. They are buried as natural human bodies, but they will be raised as spiritual bodies" (1 Cor. 15:43–44 NLT).

Anything that can be called a "body" has physical characteristics. A "spiritual body" doesn't mean ghostly or ethereal. It means our bodies will not sin, die, disease, or decay. They will be able to generate only godliness. Our eyes will never lust, our tongues will never lie, and our hands will never hit others.

Christians have debated as to what form Christ-believers will have between death and the resurrection. This stage of our existence is sometimes called the "intermediate state," i.e., the time in heaven after death before we get our new resurrected bodies. When a Christian dies, his spirit goes to be with Jesus, where he immediately experiences incredible joy. At the resurrection the "dust" of our dead body is raised out of the grave, miraculously transformed, and joined to our spirits.

Some have suggested that we will have a temporary body of some sort in this intermediate state. Once, when Jesus was transfigured on a high mountain, Moses and Elijah of the Old Testament era appeared with him in bodies that were visible to the three disciples with Jesus (Luke 9:28–36). If we can judge from this incident, believers in the intermediate state awaiting the resurrection have some kind of bodies suited for heaven.

FOR FURTHER STUDY

Luke 16:19–31; John 5:28–29; Acts 10:41; 24:15; 1 Corinthians 15:12–20, 35–49; James 2:26; 1 John 3:1–2

28 Will we live with the angels in heaven?

I n one of the most loved Christmas movies, *It's a Wonderful Life*, an angel named Clarence comes down from heaven to help a despondent businessman named George Bailey. Clarence is presented as a man who became an angel and hopes to earn his angel wings. I love the movie, but it's important to remember that the Bible always distinguishes angels from people. People don't become angels. People are still people in eternity.

The writer of the book of Hebrews asks, "Are not all angels ministering spirits sent to serve those who will inherit salvation?" (Heb. 1:14). Angels are sent by God to serve Christian believers. The evil angels fell into sin before the creation of the world. They are called demons or evil spirits in the Bible. The remaining angels are the good angels who constantly serve God's purposes. There is no salvation provided for the fallen angels or for Satan, the leader of the evil angels (or demons; 2:14–16).

One way angels serve believers is to escort them to heaven at the moment of death. In a story Jesus told about a poor beggar named Lazarus, he explained that "the time came when the beggar died and the angels carried him to Abraham's side" (Luke 16:22). (For "Abraham's side," see question #34.)

Hallmark cards may picture cute baby angels. But there are no baby angels in the Bible. Neither do angels have wings, and they certainly do not earn wings. A separate group of angelic-like beings, the seraphim, are described as having wings. But they have six wings (Isa. 6:1–2) rather than two, and are never said to earn their wings. People are also never described as having wings in heaven. Additionally, angels don't marry and don't have children (Matt.

22:30). So the number of angels cannot increase beyond the fixed number God originally created.

Angels will exist eternally like people, and Christians in heaven will live together with angels and will worship together there. The apostle John wrote of his out-of-the-body visit to heaven, "All the angels were standing around the throne and around the elders [Christian believers] and the four living creatures. They fell down on their faces before the throne and worshiped God" (Rev. 7:11). Angels can talk and communicate with people. John spoke with angels several times when he was caught up into heaven, and they spoke with him. They have individual names, although only two—Gabriel and Michael—are mentioned in the Bible.

Angels have access to earth when assigned a special task for the Lord. Gabriel came to earth to announce to Mary the birth of Jesus as Israel's Messiah (Luke 1:26–38). Angels will also be powerful forces at the end of the age when they gather God's chosen followers together and separate them from the wicked people who will be judged. Such tasks are not assigned to believing Christians while on earth, in the present heaven, or in the eternal heaven.

When angels visit earth to carry out God's personal instructions, they are able to materialize as human people. The writer of Hebrews instructs, "Do not forget to show hospitality to strangers, for by so doing some people have shown hospitality to angels without knowing it" (13:2). While angels are able to visit the present earth on God's directives, this is impossible and apparently forbidden for those who have died and gone to heaven.

Angelic beings are currently more powerful than people. But this will not be our relationship with angels in heaven. The book of Hebrews informs us, "What is man, that you are mindful of him, or the son of man, that you care for him? You made him for a little while lower than the angels" (2:6–7 ESV). "For a little while lower than the angels" refers to the time of mankind on earth. But in eternity, this will be reversed. We will be ruling over and superior to angels. This is the absolute grace of God—that he would take sinful but forgiven human people and place them over angels who have never acted in rebellion against him.

Psalm 34:7; 103:20–21; Matthew 13:49–50; 22:30; 24:31; Acts 5:19–20; 1 Timothy 5:21; Revelation 4:8

29 What is the difference between reincarnation and resurrection?

Generally, we think of evolution as a development of modern science. Actually, one form of evolution has been around for many centuries. Eastern religions, such as Buddhism and Hinduism, and modern New Age teachings speak of reincarnation as an "evolution" of the soul by transmigration. Immediately after death, a soul is recycled into another, usually better, body. Death is an illusion since it merely leads to many succeeding lifetimes. Reincarnation also teaches that people have had numerous past lives.

A person may reincarnate from an animal to a human body, or may reincarnate "downward" from a human body into an animal or insect body. For this reason, those who hold strictly to reincarnation will not kill any animal, even a fly. The law of karma, a law of good works versus bad works, determines how one will spend the next reincarnation. If she has done evil works, she may return in a body that suffers or has physical or mental handicaps. Because of this belief, there is little compassion for the disabled in some Eastern religions. Such people are merely paying for the evil of their past life or lives.

In contrast, the Bible teaches that God is a loving and forgiving God. One is never resurrected to eternal life by his good works. Forgiveness and eternal life are only possible through the grace of God, and are received by faith in Jesus' death and resurrection on their behalf. (See questions #1 and #2.)

Instead of nearly endless reincarnations, the Bible states clearly that "people are destined to die once, and after that to face judgment" (Heb. 9:27). Reincarnation suggests that we have infinite time to refine and perfect the life process. But resurrection teaches that we have just one life to live, and that life must be used for the one true God who created it.

In most teachings of reincarnation, a person must become enlightened by emptying the mind through meditation. The Bible teaches that meditation is the filling of the mind with the Word of God and with prayer. This is the opposite of emptying of the mind. Psalm 119:15 says, "I meditate on your precepts and consider your ways."

In reincarnation, a person can escape the body and become absorbed into the Divine Principle of the universe. This process obliterates individual personality by teaching that all can become blended into the One. But the Bible does not teach that the body in itself is evil. Jesus says that the mind or heart is the central problem with people, not the body itself. The body is not the penalty for sin; "the wages of sin is death" (Rom. 6:23).

Resurrection highlights individuality. A person's own body is raised up from death to join the soul (or spirit) that was previously living in it. Resurrection promises that the believer's own body will be radically transformed into a new, incorruptible, glorified, physical body prepared for a glorious new earth. Jesus did not reincarnate; he resurrected. The body that lived among the disciples and died on the cross was the same body that the disciples witnessed in his resurrection. After the resurrection, Jesus appeared to the disciples and said, "Look at my hands and my feet. It is I myself! Touch me and see . . ." (Luke 24:39).

The Bible also strictly distinguishes animals from human beings. We didn't reincarnate from an animal in the past, nor will we migrate to an animal's body in the future. When God created all the animals, he said, "Let the land produce living creatures according to their kinds: the livestock, the creatures that move along the ground, and the wild animals, each according to its kind" (Gen. 1:24).

The phrase "according to its kind" or an equivalent is repeated ten times in the creation account of Genesis 1. Not only were people made distinct from animals, people were made in the image of God, not animals. The image of God comprises a built-in moral understanding and ethical responsibility that animals don't have.

According to the Bible, the resurrection of the body will take place both for the one who has believed in Christ and goes to heaven and the one who rejects Christ and goes to hell. Paul said that there will be a "resurrection of both the righteous and the wicked" (Acts 24:15). So everyone's body will be prepared in a resurrection for an eternal punishment or an eternal delight in God's presence.

FOR FURTHER STUDY

Isaiah 26:19; Daniel 12:2; Luke 20:35–36; John 5:25–29; 9:1–7; Acts 17:18; 1 Corinthians 15:42–44; Revelation 20:4–6

30 Will everyone be alike in heaven?

Every individual human being is a creation of God, whom he made extensively unique. Today, biometric identifications that are distinctive to every person include their fingerprints, their teeth (dental records), their DNA, and perhaps even their iris and tongue.

Although identical twins were once thought by scientists to have matching DNA, recent studies have disproved this proposal. It is true that no one person is identical to any other person, even in their DNA.

One's DNA and fingerprints demonstrate that God's creativity cannot be exhausted. He delights in diversity, but with unity. That's how God made our bodies: many different parts working in unity. Paul wrote, "If the whole body were an eye, where would the sense of hearing be? If the whole body were an ear, where would the sense of smell be? But in fact God has placed the parts in the body, every one of them, just as he wanted them to be. If they were all one part, where would the body be?" (1 Cor. 12:17–19). Paul used the physical body to illustrate how God made each individual believer different, with different spiritual gifts or talents. Yet each believer is to work together as a unit with all other true believers. This distinctiveness of each person will be retained in our eternal, resurrected bodies.

Although everyone in heaven will be sinless (perfect), it doesn't require that everyone be identical in our personalities or responsibilities. At creation, God made both male and female after his own image (Gen. 1:27). Adam and Eve were both created sinless (perfect) in the garden of Eden. Yet they were not identical, even in gender. Undoubtedly, their personalities were different. So were their responsibilities. A woman on earth will be a woman in heaven, and a man on earth will be a man in heaven.

We will all have our individual names in heaven as well. Jesus said that he is like a good shepherd who has named his sheep. Believers are his sheep, and he "calls his own sheep by name" (John 10:3). We will not just blend into a mass of humanity or be assigned a number for our identification in heaven. Social security numbers will be obsolete. Moses and Peter will be called in heaven what they were called on earth. Our name is part of our identity, making us a distinct individual, different from all others. Jesus certainly did not lose the name "Jesus" after his resurrection.

When we come to faith, our names are written in the book of life in heaven.

When Jesus met Mary after his resurrection, she did not recognize him at first because she was crying and looking away. But when he called her by her name, Mary, "She turned toward him and cried out . . . 'Teacher!'" (John 20:16). The exact tone of his voice sent a signal by which she recognized him. Perhaps even the tone of our voice may not change in heaven. Jesus was also identified after his resurrection as the same distinct individual his disciples knew before the resurrection. We too will be identifiable as the same person others knew on earth.

Everyone's body will be fully developed but youthful and ageless. At the beginning, God created Adam and Eve with a developed adult body without having them pass through a physical maturing process. Without the entrance of sin, they would have remained at this peak of physical maturity. This was God's archetype for humanity. So children who have come to faith in Christ but have died before adulthood will be full grown in their resurrected bodies. Those who have died at an old age will be resurrected into a premier adult body. There will be no gray hair or baldness, no teeth that are missing, no replacement joints, no memory loss, and no need for glasses or contacts.

I'm short in height when compared to other men in our culture. But I don't expect to be any taller in heaven. God has no one height or one body build for people. We will never long to be taller or shorter, thinner or heavier—although in our resurrected body God may trim a few pounds from some of us, and add a few to others.

Our renewed minds in heaven will not even think in these earthly terms. We will love everyone as they are, with absolutely no thoughts about their shape, size, color, appearance, or build. Each of us will reflect the glory of Christ, and we will consider everyone *unusually* beautiful. All disabilities will disappear. No missing limbs, no deformities, no paralysis, no blindness, no scars. Only Jesus will have scars—the scar in his side and the nail prints in his hands. These will be the eternal reminder of his crucifixion for our sins.

FOR FURTHER STUDY

Genesis 25:21–27; John 20:25–27; Romans 12:4–8; 1 Corinthians 12:20–21; 15:22, 45; Revelation 20:15; 21:27

31 Will there be any sin in heaven?

Does any great rescue story end with the princess being recaptured and killed? Would the handsome prince have revived Snow White from her glass coffin and married her, only to allow the evil queen to poison her once again? Impossible! Would Superman rescue Lois Lane, only to leave her weak and defenseless so as to be kidnapped again? Not likely. Would Luke Skywalker rescue Princess Leia only to allow Darth Vader to reclaim her? Not Luke Skywalker! And Jesus won't allow his bride, Christian believers, to be recaptured by sin in heaven after he has suffered a torturous death on earth to rescue them from sin forever.

When Adam and Eve first brought sin into the world of people, they were tempted and enticed by Satan, the leader-angel of the evil spirit world. So the first thing that God will do to prevent the return of sin into the world will be to powerfully and permanently confine Satan. Then he will never be able to tempt another person again. God told John in his vision of the future, "And the devil, who deceived them [the people of earth], was thrown into the lake of burning sulfur. . . . [He] will be tormented day and night for ever and ever" (Rev. 20:10). Satan will never escape the lake of fire, so he will never again tempt another person for all eternity.

When Adam and Eve first disobeyed God's command in the garden, God said they would die. Death was and is the penalty for sin. The early chapters of Genesis, the first book of the Bible, trace how, one after another, every person died who was born after the first couple sinned. Death pervades the narrative of Genesis. In the New Testament, Paul said it this way: "For the wages of sin is death" (Rom. 6:23).

If we could sin in heaven, even after billions of years on the new earth, then death would have to follow. Sin leads to death. But Revelation 21:4 states that God "will wipe every tear from their eyes. There will be no more death or mourning or crying or pain, for the old order of things has passed away." "No more death" means that there will be no more sin that leads to death. Why? Because the "old order of things has passed away." Death, and the mourning, crying, and pain that come with it, are part of the old order that will pass away. In the new order of things, death will not exist. That means sin will never exist either.

What happens when you "abolish" something? Synonyms for "abolish" include *eliminate, obliterate,* and *eradicate.* These are strong words. But that's what Jesus did with death. He "has abolished death and has brought life and immortality to light through the gospel" (2 Tim. 1:10 NKJV). Immortality means to be exempt from death. Where there is no death, neither is there sin. The Bible also says that at the resurrection, "the trumpet will sound, the dead will be raised imperishable, and we will be changed" (1 Cor. 15:52). "Imperishable" indicates never dying, everlasting, and indestructible. If there were the possibility of sin in heaven, then there would be the possibility that God could curse the new earth like he did the present earth when sin entered the universe. But instead he has promised, "No longer will there be any curse" (Rev. 22:3).

There will be no temptation in heaven either. Once the first couple sinned, a strong sinful tendency was generated in each person and has been passed on to everyone through all of history. The apostle Paul called this sinful inclination "the flesh." He didn't mean the body or the tissue on our bones. He was talking about the powerful force inside all humans that draws us away from God and his laws for us.

The book of James discusses how "each person is tempted when they are dragged away by their own evil desire and enticed. Then, after desire has conceived, it gives birth to sin . . ." (1:14–15). In heaven we won't have those evil desires, and therefore we won't sin. There will never be the temptation to be envious, bitter, lustful, controlling, harsh, proud, or selfish. What desires tend to pull you away from God? Think of it. You, as a Christ-believer, will never have those alluring attractions in heaven.

In the resurrection, God promised we will be like Jesus. The Christian has been chosen by God and "predestined to be conformed to the image of his Son" (Rom. 8:29). God determined ahead of time that in heaven the believer will be like Jesus—sinless. So if anyone in heaven could sin, then God would not conform us to his Son. In eternity made like Jesus, we will never sin again.

FOR FURTHER STUDY

Romans 6:7; 1 Corinthians 15:49; Philippians 3:20–21; Hebrews 10:10, 14; 1 John 3:1–2; Revelation 21:27

32 Will we eat and drink in heaven?

An elderly couple died and went to heaven. When told they could eat anything they wanted and not gain weight or get sick, the husband told his wife, "If you hadn't stressed healthy eating so much, I could have been here ten years earlier!"

Someone has said that there will be no fast foods in heaven because no one will be in a hurry. But neither will there be a need for health foods in heaven. No one will be eating healthy to live longer. Nor will anyone count calories, go on a diet, or eat special foods to avoid allergies. The real question is, If we do not need to eat to stay alive and healthy, will we eat at all in heaven?

In every culture and nationality, eating a meal together is intimately connected with friendship, companionship, conversation, and hospitality. In Israel the seven major religious celebrations were called "Feasts" because nearly all included major times of festive eating. These times of eating commemorated God's faithfulness to and communion with his people.

The first miracle Jesus ever did took place at a wedding in Cana in Galilee (northern Israel). Wedding celebrations in the Jewish culture of that time often lasted seven days. That's a lot of eating and drinking! At some point in the celebration, the wine at the wedding ran out. Jesus had the servants fill six empty stone jars with water. The jars were huge, containing about twenty to thirty gallons each. Once they were filled to the brim, Jesus instantly turned them into aged wine. It tasted far superior to any wine the guests had had so far. The purpose of this miracle was to symbolize the eternal kingdom Jesus would establish on the new earth after his second coming. The abundance of wine pictured the abundance of joy in that kingdom.

Not only will we eat in heaven, it will be central to the celebration of Jesus' return to establish his rulership over the world. At Christ's return, prophesied by John, the announcement is made, "Let us rejoice and exult and give him [God] glory, because the wedding celebration of the Lamb [Jesus] has come, and his bride [all Christian believers] has made herself ready" (Rev. 19:7 NET). This celebration, like most weddings in our own culture, will include a wedding banquet. An angel told John to write down this promise: "Blessed are those who are invited to the banquet at the wedding celebration of the Lamb!" (v. 19:9 NET). What is a banquet if there is no food and drink?

The night before Jesus' death, he celebrated the Passover by sharing a meal with his disciples. Then he broke some bread into pieces and ate it with them. This act represented how, by faith, believers are joined spiritually with Jesus' broken body, which was crucified on the cross.

Next he took a cup of wine, and together they drank it. This represented his blood that was spilled out while on the cross. Finally he said, "Truly I tell you, I will not drink again from the fruit of the vine until that day when I drink it new in the kingdom of God" (Mark 14:25). If Jesus and his disciples will eat and drink in the coming kingdom, so will all who have put their faith in him.

On one occasion, when a Roman (Gentile) military leader asked Jesus to come heal his servant, Jesus explained to those following him that many other people outside Judaism would eat in his coming kingdom. "I say to you that many will come from the east and the west, and will take their places at the feast with Abraham, Isaac and Jacob in the kingdom of heaven" (Matt. 8:11).

After his resurrection, Jesus himself ate with his disciples on at least three occasions. Since his resurrection body is a pattern for ours, we too will eat in our resurrection bodies in the eternal heaven. Jesus even taught his disciples directly that he would eat and drink with them in his kingdom rule. He told them, "you may eat and drink at my table in my kingdom and sit on thrones, judging the twelve tribes of Israel" (Luke 22:30).

Since our bodies will be perfect and will not need the food we eat, everything that is eaten will be completely absorbed into our bodies or miraculously disappear inside us. There will be no need for any elimination of liquids or solids. Nothing will come out too fast or too slow since nothing will need to come out at all! For many of us, happy day! No acid reflux, indigestion, food poisoning, or other such issues. We will eat all the hot sauce and spicy food we want!

FOR FURTHER STUDY

Isaiah 25:6; Matthew 22:1–4; 25:10; Luke 22:17–18; 24:30, 41–43; John 21:12–13; Acts 10:41; Revelation 2:7

33 What does the Bible say about hell?

While most people would probably say that they don't believe hell exists, it shows up repeatedly in their conversations. "What the hell are you doing?" "That place is a hell on earth." "Go to hell!" "Hell no!" If hell doesn't exist, why do we repeatedly speak of it or tell people to go there? Jesus also used the word *hell* in his conversations. But he clearly believed that it exists and warned people of its severe punishment. In fact, Jesus used the word more frequently by far than any other writer or speaker in the Bible.

All Christians who affirm the Bible as true agree that the teachings about hell are the most difficult of all to understand and accept. A few years ago a well-known Christian leader wrote a book called *Love Wins*. Although he originally held that the Bible spoke of a future punishment in hell, he had now changed his mind. God was too loving a God to punish people for eternity. God's character includes more than just love; he is also righteous, holy, and just.

But hypothetically, a judge's son who has committed several heinous murders could appear in court before his father to be sentenced. No matter how much the father might love his son, as a judge he would be constrained to follow the law and sentence his son to a severe punishment, otherwise he would be disqualified as a judge. So it is with God. Although he deeply loves all people, he is a righteous judge. Love cannot overrule his role as judge. If it did, he would be disqualified as God and judge. He must follow the moral laws of right and wrong he has set in the universe.

The main word in the New Testament translated "hell" is *gehenna*. The word is derived from the Valley of Hinnom, located on the south side of Jerusalem. This valley was a place where human excrement, trash, the dead bodies of animals, and executed criminals were burned. The fires there were kept burning continually in attempts to destroy the worm-infested garbage. In the time of Jesus, the name *gehenna* came to be used of the place of everlasting suffering and divine punishment.

So what did Jesus say about gehenna or hell? First, he spoke of its endlessness. Hell is a place "where worms don't die and the fire never goes out" (Mark 9:48 CEB). Jesus was actually quoting from the final words of the prophet Isaiah (Isa. 66:24). His teaching on hell was not much different from the Jewish Old Testament.

Some people interpret the word *eternal* to mean "ages." They insist that the original word only meant "ages" (a time period), and ages are not eternal. But *eternal* is used of God's character. He is "the eternal God" (Rom. 16:26). Also, in telling a parable about wicked and righteous people, Jesus said, "Then they will go away to eternal punishment, but the righteous to eternal life" (Matt. 25:46). So if hell isn't eternal, neither is heaven. Verses like this also eliminate the possibility that everyone will eventually be in heaven.

Several Bible passages contain dreadful descriptions of hell. "And the smoke of their torment will rise for ever and ever. There will be no rest day or night . . ." (Rev. 14:11). No wonder Jesus warned, "Do not be afraid of those who kill the body but cannot kill the soul. Rather, be afraid of the One who can destroy both soul and body in hell" (Matt. 10:28).

Jesus also spoke of God's intent in creating hell. From the very beginning, hell was never designed for people. God never desired to send people to hell. It was originally designed to punish the fallen angels (i.e., demons). Nevertheless, Jesus will one day say to those who are wicked, "Depart from me, you who are cursed, into the eternal fire prepared for the devil and his angels" (Matt. 25:41).

It seems unfair that God would punish people eternally for things that were done in a lifetime. This is certainly difficult to comprehend. Perhaps part of the answer is that we cannot fully comprehend the abominable nature of sin. We might think it the height of evil for Hitler to murder millions of Jews and thousands of others. But to God, the "little lie" we told might be the same to him as the evil of Hitler is to us. A person might use a racial slur in a casual conversation, thinking nothing of it. But this does not account for the pain such words can cause for other people. Our "little sins" are BIG to God.

Will people be repentant or sorrowful for their sins in hell? I don't think so. The character of unbelieving people will not have changed. Immoral people in hell will still be immoral, ever controlled by selfish lusts. The hateful will continue to be hateful, unchanged by their punishment. The final chapter of the Bible speaks of eternity this way: "Evil people will keep on being evil, and everyone who is dirty-minded will still be dirty-minded" (Rev. 22:11 CEV). This is one reason that an eternal punishment is just and right for those who refuse to accept Jesus as Savior. Sin will continue unabated in hell. Bitterness and hatred toward God will still characterize the unbeliever's true nature.

All those who have rejected faith in Jesus will stand before the Judge of the whole earth. In Revelation 20:11–15, this judgment is called the great white throne judgment (see question #45). Second Thessalonians 1:8 (NET) says, "With flaming fire he [Jesus] will mete out punishment on those who do not know God and do not obey the gospel of our Lord Jesus."

FOR FURTHER STUDY

Ezekiel 33:11; Matthew 8:12; 10:28; John 3:36; Romans 2:4–11; 2 Peter 3:7–10; Revelation 4:8–11; 20:10, 14–15

34 What do the words *Sheol* and *Hades* refer to?

It may be a surprise to know that according to the Bible no one is in hell yet. Our modern culture uses the term *hell* to refer to the final place of punishment. The Bible actually calls the place of final judgment the "lake of fire." No one is in the lake of fire yet. The book of Revelation records a vision the apostle John had of the final judgment at the very end of all human history. At this judgment, "anyone whose name was not found written in the book of life was thrown into the lake of fire" (20:15). But this is not until the future, final judgment.

In the Old Testament Hebrew language, the place of the departed dead was called "Sheol." The King James Version translated this word as "hell." Most modern versions of the Bible simply transliterate this Hebrew word as "Sheol" or translate it as "grave" or "death." This is because *Sheol* is 1) sometimes used to mean only death or the grave, and 2) other times used for the residence of those who have died without faith in the God of Israel (Ps. 9:17). The faithful in Israel are delivered from this latter "Sheol" (Ps. 49:14–15; 73:23–24).

When the ancient Greek translation was made of the Old Testament Hebrew Bible (ca. 150 BC), the translators used the Greek word "Hades" for the Hebrew word *Sheol*. Jesus used this Greek word, *Hades*, in one of the stories he told (Luke 16).

The story is about two men who had died. One was a poor man named Lazarus (not to be confused with the Lazarus who was raised from the dead by Jesus in John 11). The other was an unnamed, greedy rich man. After both had died, Lazarus went to "Abraham's bosom," or Abraham's side (Luke 16:22), an expression picturing close friendship with the faithful forefather of God's people. "Abraham's bosom" is a picture of heaven or paradise. This is reflected in the well-known spiritual, "Rocka My Soul in the Bosom of Abraham."

In the story, Abraham himself was in this place of comfort and rest (heaven). On the other hand, the rich man was in a place separated from Lazarus by a large impassible gorge (v. 23). Speaking of the rich man, Jesus said, "In Hades, where he was in torment . . ." (Luke 16:23). Hades is much like how we think of hell.

The rich man appealed to Abraham to send Lazarus so that he might dip the tip of his finger in water and cool off his (the rich man's) tongue (v. 24). But Abraham replied that it was impossible. The large chasm between them prevented anyone from traversing it in either direction (v. 26). Jesus never otherwise used the names of specific people in his parables, so the story appears to be about two real people.

Hades actually refers to a temporary place of confinement and punishment. When a criminal is captured and arrested, he is incarcerated in a local jail to await his trial. Once the trial and sentence are finalized, he is sent away to prison. So also, those who have rejected Christ are temporarily confined in a place of punishment to await their trial before the Judge of the universe. Once the sentence is pronounced, they will be confined to the lake of fire, the final imprisonment: "The Lord knows how . . . to keep the unrighteous under punishment [in Hades] for the day of judgment" (2 Peter 2:9 NASB). At the final judgment, Hades will be thrown into the lake of fire. After the final judgment, it is declared that "death and Hades were thrown into the lake of fire" (Rev. 20:14).

FOR FURTHER STUDY

Deuteronomy 32:22; Psalm 89:48; Isaiah 38:10; Acts 2:25–27; Revelation 20:11–15

35 Are the stories true about people going to heaven and returning? Are the stories of near-death experiences true? Have people come back from heaven?

A simple search of the Internet will uncover numerous books in which a person claims to have died and gone to heaven. In these near-death experiences (NDEs), people often claim to have been lifted out of their bodies, to have seen stunning, beautiful light brighter than the sun, and to have met large groups of transparent, shimmering beings. But search results of the Internet will also find the opposite experiences. For example, I found one book in which the author claims he died and went to hell, only to be brought back to life to serve God. Another book claims that numerous people who have reported NDEs have recanted their testimony after scrutiny. How can we know who's telling the truth? How can we know if these experiences are real?

We must remember that all such experiences are not actually experiences of the afterlife but resuscitations before the finality of death. Who has been pronounced dead by official sources, laid dead for a week, then come back to life to tell about it? How can we be sure that these experiences of "near death" will be the same as those of real death? Apart from a supernatural miracle, the Bible states that death for each person happens only once. "People are destined to die once, and after that to face judgment" (Heb. 9:27).

There is a story in the New Testament about a friend of Jesus named Lazarus who died and was buried. When Jesus arrived at the tomb, he asked that the stone over the opening be rolled away. Martha, one of Lazarus's sisters, insisted that her brother had been dead four days and opening the tomb would produce a horrific stench. But at Jesus' instructions they rolled the stone away, and Lazarus came out with his graveclothes still on (John 11:39–44).

This was an unparalleled, miraculous resurrection. What's interesting is that Lazarus tells no stories of his experience in the grave, or what it was like to be dead and go to heaven (he had believed in Jesus). If he recited to others some details about a heavenly visit, the disciples of Jesus (including John, who wrote this story) never felt they were important enough to record in Scripture.

The apostle Paul himself had a near-death experience in which he "was caught up to paradise [heaven]." What he saw and heard was absolutely incredible. He "heard inexpressible things, things that no one is permitted to tell" (2 Cor. 12:4). He maintained after his heavenly visit that God gave him a "thorn in the flesh" (a physical affliction) to keep him humble. If that was the case for this key New Testament leader of the church, it seems unlikely that God would allow someone else to experience a departure to heaven and come back to tell about it. Don't many of these NDEs bring more attention to the participant than to the heavenly experience itself?

Many near-death testimonies contradict each other, and contradict the teachings of the Bible as well. They are often used to support a philosophical or religious viewpoint that the person had while alive. Frequently, experiences of the Great Beyond are reported by those who have participated in occult practices strictly forbidden by the Bible. Evil spirit beings (demons) are often behind such experiences. Paul warned one of the churches he established that "Satan himself masquerades as an angel of light" (2 Cor. 11:14). Stories of seeing brilliant light do not automatically mean that spiritual teachings drawn from such stories are reliable.

Some information about the spirit world and life after death is not meant for us to know yet. Moses told the people of Israel, "The secret things belong to the LORD our God, but the things revealed belong to us" (Deut. 29:29). We are to focus on what God tells us in the Bible, not on experiences that individuals have had in NDEs. We are instructed to live by faith and not by physical sight (2 Cor. 5:7).

Jesus himself suffered death and was raised to tell about it. Shouldn't his testimony be worthy of our trust? Saint Peter has no keys to the pearly gates. Jesus alone has those keys. He said, "Do not be afraid. I am the First and the Last. I am the Living One; I was dead, and now look, I am alive for ever and ever! And I hold the keys of death and Hades" (Rev. 1:17–18).

FOR FURTHER STUDY

Leviticus 19:31; Deuteronomy 18:10–12; Mark 9:1–10; 2 Corinthians 12:2–8; 2 Peter 2:1–3

36 Don't other religions have a similar teaching to the Bible's teaching about heaven?

This question is like asking, "Aren't tigers very much like kitty cats?" While there are certainly many characteristics of tigers that parallel domestic kittens, the contrasts far outweigh the comparisons. The Bible's teachings on heaven have some similarities to other religions, but the contrasts are substantial and numerous.

The most dramatic dissimilarity between the Christian faith and all other religious systems is in the condition(s) by which one gets to paradise or heaven in the afterlife. The Bible makes it repeatedly clear that faith alone (just one condition) brings a person into a right relationship with God. This faith must be placed in Jesus as the only one who can give eternal life. Jesus said, "I am the way and the truth and the life. No one comes to the Father except through me" (John 14:6). (See questions #1 and #2.)

All other religious groups—for instance, Islam, Judaism, Hinduism—teach that good works (some form of moral/ethical living) along with faith in their teachings (two conditions) gain one entrance into paradise. The Qur'an states, "As for those that have faith *and do good works* and humble themselves before their Lord, they are the heirs of Paradise . . ." (Sura 11:23, italics added). Various minor groups that claim the Christian faith, such as Jehovah's Witnesses and Mormons, also emphasize both good works and a moral lifestyle in order to get to heaven.

Good works and faith in Jesus are the conditions given for heaven within Roman Catholicism and Eastern Orthodox Christianity, distinguishing them from most of evangelical Protestant Christianity. The apostle Paul addressed this issue: "God saved you by his grace when you believed. And you can't take credit for this; it is a gift from God. Salvation is not a reward for the good things we have done, so none of us can boast about it" (Eph. 2:8–9 NLT).

In Islamic faith, heaven is pictured as a paradise or garden of Eden with wonderful fruits and flowing rivers. Paradise is gained by following diligently the five pillars of Islam: faith in Allah as the only God and Muhammad as his messenger; five ritual prayers each day; almsgiving; fasting during Ramadan, the ninth month of the Islamic calendar; and pilgrimage to Mecca (if at all possible). Heaven is composed of various levels (seven or eight) providing different degrees of comfort. The highest heaven is reserved for the elite who are chosen by Allah, such as the prophet Muhammad.

According to the Bible, there are no varying degrees of heaven. Everyone who genuinely believes in Jesus will live with Jesus forever in the highest comfort and deepest happiness. No one in heaven will be excluded from being personally in the presence of God.

In contrast to the teachings of Jesus, Islam claims that there will be marriage in heaven. (See question #19.) In paradise all the longings and passions of this life will be fulfilled. The Qur'an and other Islamic sources describe men in heaven as having multiple wives involving lustful pleasures. But according to the Bible, all sinful desires will disappear in heaven.

Christianity is monotheistic. But some groups within Hinduism are pantheistic and others are polytheistic. Christians believe in a bodily resurrection, but Hindus believe in reincarnation, i.e., a migration of the soul to a new body (animal or human) after death. (For the differences between resurrection and reincarnation, see question #29.)

Some Hindus believe in many gods and conduct priestly rituals and sacrifices. Others hold to one single divine reality called Brahman, an impersonal force that is part of every living person. In this latter form of Hinduism, there is no "heaven." Instead, the goal of life is to escape the cycle of reincarnation by suppressing individual consciousness and uniting with the one Divine Principle of the universe. This is achieved by mindless meditation and forms of yoga designed to lose one's individual identity and blend with Brahman. Heaven is not a place but a state of the soul or self. "Hell" is existing in a physical body and continuing in the cycle of reincarnation.

Buddhism shares some common beliefs with Hinduism yet is nontheistic. The Buddha taught that there is no eternal god. Buddhism rejects both resurrection and reincarnation because it does not believe in a "soul" of an individual. Since there is no eternal self or soul, there is no heaven or hell either. The self is made up of "parts" that rearrange themselves as a "rebirth" in a new life-form. Impermanent gods exist, but they also need to escape rebirth like us. Although this rebirth seems similar to reincarnation, Buddhists reject reincarnation because they do not believe in a soul.

In Hinduism, "nirvana" (i.e., a state of pure happiness, a "heaven") is reached when one blends completely with the Divine Principle. In Buddhism, nirvana is reached when the "self" and all desires are extinguished through asceticism or meditation. The goal of life is to lose all appetites and desires. Our desires lead to suffering. So to eliminate suffering, one must deny all longings.

The Bible, however, affirms that God created every individual to exist eternally. He also placed within us many desires that, when one is yielded to God, are pure and holy. When one is spiritually united to Jesus by faith, his individual identity is renewed, not obliterated. Suffering is caused by the entrance of sin in the universe. Christians are called to deny sinful longings, not all longings.

FOR FURTHER STUDY

Matthew 5:8; 10:29–31; Romans 15:23; Galatians 5:22–24; Philippians 2:1–3; Titus 3:5; Revelation 21:27

37 Is anyone just annihilated at death?

Are all people immortal? Will all people, regardless of faith or morality, exist forever? Some religious groups and people hold that not every person is immortal, i.e., not every person will consciously live forever, particularly in hell. Instead, God will simply annihilate (i.e., make eternally nonexistent) those who don't come to faith in Jesus Christ. Such people just cease to exist. This religious belief, called annihilationism, holds that there is no immortality for such people.

Many who hold to annihilationism believe that people are not created immortal but only receive immortality after faith in Jesus. They insist that only God is immortal, not people. After all, 1 Timothy 6:16 says that God is the one "who alone is immortal." Immortality is not innate to humanity. God did not create people with endless life. So, they reason, when a person dies who has refused to accept Jesus Christ as Savior, he or she is resurrected to face God's judgment. This person's judgment will be eternal eradication.

It is true that the word *immortality* in the Bible is reserved only for God and those who have faith in his Son. But this is not because immortality is a gift that God gives only to the ones who go to heaven. In our English language, *immortality* means just an endless existence, nothing more. The word *immortality* in the Bible is used only of a specific kind of endless existence—a stupendous quality of life with an unrivaled joy and happiness. The unbeliever does not "live forever" in *that* sense. The endless existence of the unbeliever cannot be called "life" since God's kind of "life" is an experience that comes only when a person has a relationship with him.

The Bible actually calls the unbeliever's eternal existence "the second death" (Rev. 20:14; 21:8). The "first" death is our physical death. It is the separation of our spirit (or soul) from our body. The second death is also a separation—an eternal separation from the presence of God. Paul said that God "will punish those who do not know God and do not obey the gospel of our Lord Jesus. They will be punished with everlasting destruction and shut out from the presence of the Lord" (2 Thess. 1:8–9). The Bible cannot call this experience life. It can only call it death. So for the one who does not receive Jesus Christ as Savior, there is no life after death. There is death after death. *Eternal life* is a term used only for those who believe in the Son of God. Others experience eternal death.

Another passage that is used to support annihilationism is Jesus' teaching in Matthew 10:28: "Do not be afraid of those who kill the body but cannot kill the soul. Rather, be afraid of the One who can destroy both soul and body in hell." A quick reading of the verse seems to suggest that the soul of a person (his true inner self) is annihilated (i.e., destroyed) in hell.

Several other passages speak of God's "destruction" of the wicked (Phil. 3:19; 1 Thess. 5:3; 2 Thess. 1:9; 2 Peter 3:7). But the words used for destroying someone like the one in Matthew 10:28 do not mean to make nonexistent but to ruin. On one occasion, some expensive perfume was poured on Jesus' feet (Matt. 26:8).

The disciples called this a "waste" of the perfume, using the same root word for "destroy" as in Matthew 10:28. But the perfume wasn't annihilated.

God intended all people to love him and worship him. In this life they choose to do or not do this. Their choice sets their eternal destiny. To choose not to know God through Jesus is to become "ruined" in hell, a waste of what their life was meant to be.

In most teachings of annihilationism, no suffering is ever experienced in eternity, by any sinner. The punishment is identical for all, even for the worst of humanity like a Hitler or a Stalin. There are no degrees of punishment. This kind of justice does not seem to be justice after all. But many passages in the Bible speak of the eternal suffering of those who have refused to accept Christ's forgiveness. For example, John predicted the coming of an evil world ruler called "the beast." Anyone who worships him will be "tormented with burning sulfur in the presence of the holy angels and of the Lamb. And the smoke of their torment will rise for ever and ever" (Rev. 14:10–11).

FOR FURTHER STUDY

Matthew 3:12; 18:8; 25:31–46; Mark 9:42–48; 2 Thessalonians 1:8; Jude 6–7; Revelation 20:10

38 Is there such a thing as soul sleep?

Soul sleep" is the perspective held by some that according to the Bible, the soul (or spirit) of every dead person is unconscious or "sleeps" until the resurrection. Those who hold this view maintain that the repeated use of the word *sleep* for the dead supports this belief. For example, Jesus said of Lazarus who had died in Bethany, "Our friend Lazarus has fallen asleep; but I am going there to wake him up" (John 11:11).

It is true that many passages in the Bible speak of death as "sleep" (e.g., Dan. 12:2; Matt. 9:24; 1 Thess. 4:13–16). Like Jesus, Paul also spoke of death as sleep. "Listen," he said. "I tell you a mystery: We will not all sleep, but we will all be changed" (1 Cor. 15:51). He was explaining how believers who are alive at the final return of Jesus will not die ("sleep") and their bodies decay, but will be immediately transformed by a resurrection at Christ's return. Resurrection raises a dead body back to life; resurrection does not awaken the soul, which is still living after death.

However, passages about death as "sleep" must be read in light of many other clear passages that show that people are not asleep or unconscious after death. The Bible describes death as "sleep" because this is how we on earth see a person's dead body. We ourselves often use the language of appearance, such as when we say things like "the sun is rising."

The deceased lie motionless like someone who is asleep. It is the body that is asleep, not the soul. In Luke 16:19–31, Jesus told a story of a certain poor man named Lazarus, an unnamed rich man, and Abraham, all of whom he described as fully conscious after death. They were able to see, talk, and remember the past, and were fully aware of their surroundings (see this story also in questions #3 and #34).

On the cross, Jesus told one of the criminals who was crucified with him and had expressed faith, "Truly I tell you, today you will be with me in paradise" (Luke 23:43). But what comfort is a promise of paradise if we are unconscious there? Some religious groups reword this, saying, "Truly I tell you *today*, you will be with me in paradise." But why would Jesus have to explain to the criminal that he was speaking "today"? What other day would he be speaking?

In another incident in the life of Jesus, he took up on a high mountain three of his trusted disciples—Peter, James, and John.

There Jesus was transformed so that his face shone like the sun and his clothing became a brilliant white. Then both Moses and Elijah, dead for hundreds of years, appeared to all of them on the mountain. The disciples saw these two great prophets of the Old Testament consciously speaking with Jesus (Matt. 17:1–8). This certainly wasn't soul sleep.

Paul wrote to a church he founded in Philippi, "I am torn between the two: I desire to depart and be with Christ, which is better by far; but it is more necessary for you that I remain in the body" (Phil. 1:23–24). If Paul was speaking of soul sleep, he would not have viewed it as "far better." Why would he have wanted to exchange a life of conscious communion with his Lord on earth for an unconscious sleep of his soul in death? The latter would have no conscious communion with Jesus.

His desire to consciously be with Jesus after death is also reflected in other comments he makes. "We are confident, I say, and would prefer to be away from the body and at home with the Lord" (2 Cor. 5:8). Again, Paul would not prefer an unconscious "fellowship" with Jesus in heaven over a conscious fellowship with Jesus in the body. A fellowship that is unconscious is really no fellowship at all.

Revelation is filled with scenes that the apostle John saw in a vision of heaven. In every description, disembodied souls in heaven are conscious. For example, in Revelation 6:9–10, John saw "the souls of those who had been slain because of the word of God" and they cried out, "How long, Sovereign Lord, holy and true, until you . . . avenge our blood?" This hardly sounds like soul sleep.

FOR FURTHER STUDY

Psalm 73:24–26; Luke 20:34–38; 23:43; 2 Corinthians 5:1–10; 12:2–4; Hebrews 12:22–24; Revelation 6:9–11

39 Do some people go to purgatory after death?

The word *purgatory* does not appear in the Bible. Purgatory is related to our word *purge* ("cleanse") and is a teaching that after death the spirits of some people go to a temporary place of punishment and suffering where they are purged or cleansed of their sins. Once their sins are paid for and their punishment is complete, the person is released from torment and can enter heaven. The punishment may be several years or millions of years, depending on what the person did while on earth.

The teaching of purgatory arose in the late Middle Ages. Very little of this teaching can be found in the early church era. Among some Christian groups, the teaching of purgatory includes the possibility that the prayers offered, donations given, religious services attended, or other religious activities performed can reduce one's time in purgatory. These same rites can be offered also for departed loved ones, friends, or relatives so as to reduce their time in torment. But even the person who knows only a little of the Bible should see in these teachings a favoritism toward the rich, reversing Jesus' teachings that elevated the poor over the wealthy (cf. Luke 6:20; 21:1–4; James 2:5).

Second Maccabees, one of the books of the Apocrypha, is often used by certain groups to support the teaching of purgatory. *Apocrypha* is from a Greek word meaning "hidden," named because these books were thought to have hidden or secret truths. This group of writings is accepted as inspired Scripture by the Roman Catholic Church and the Orthodox Church but is rejected by all Jewish and most Protestant Scriptures. In 2 Maccabees 12:38–45, an unknown author tells of how Jewish warriors had died during battle as a result of secret acts of idolatry. Judas Maccabaeus, their leader, prayed for the dead warriors and paid for a sacrifice to be offered in Jerusalem for their sins.

Protestants reject the Apocrypha since none of its books (with one possible exception) are quoted directly in the New Testament, as are all the books of the Jewish and Protestant Old Testament Scriptures with the exception of the book of Esther.

The concept of a purgatory seemingly contradicts the rest of the New Testament's teachings on how one gets to heaven and on the finality of one's destiny after death. When Jesus died on the cross, two criminals were crucified on either side of him. One sarcastically defied Jesus. "Aren't you the Messiah? Save yourself and us!" But the other criminal rebuked him. "Don't you fear God," he said, "since you are under the same sentence? We are punished justly, for we are getting what our deeds deserve. But this man has done nothing wrong." Then he said to Jesus, "Jesus, remember me when you come into your kingdom." This second criminal, though he had done no more good deeds than the first, called with faith for Jesus to rescue him. Jesus' answer is astounding: "Truly I tell you, today you will be with me in paradise." No mention of a purgatory, only of paradise, heaven, eternal life! (This story is found in Luke 23:39–43.)

A purgatory in which people are punished only temporarily promotes a system of reward and punishment based on our goodness or the goodness of other people who work religiously on our behalf. Each person can pay for his or her own sins and even pay for the sins of another. But the Bible says the very opposite. Jesus alone has paid the penalty for all our sins. We are already purged of sin if we have faith in Jesus the Savior. First John 1:7 explains that "the blood of Jesus, his Son, purifies us from all sin." The "all" sounds radically comprehensive, and it is. This purging of our sins is without any reference to purgatory. Jesus alone can remove our guilt. God requires that we accept his way of forgiveness and believe that the penalty was completely paid by Jesus when he suffered God's wrath for us on the cross. Like the criminal who came to faith on a cross next to Jesus, the one who believes in this Savior proceeds to paradise immediately at death.

FOR FURTHER STUDY

Psalm 130:4; Jeremiah 33:8; Acts 10:43; Ephesians 1:7; Hebrews 7:27; 9:26; 10:10; 1 Peter 3:18

40 How can I explain heaven to my young children?

Will there be Legos in heaven, Dad?" I don't remember if my oldest son actually said this to me, but he certainly could have. At Christmas when he was five years old he got his first Lego set, and he has been collecting and building them ever since, even now in his thirties. A question like this is very practical for a child, and we should never reprimand a child for asking it.

I don't know how I might have answered this question when my children were young. But I know what I would say now. My answer would be, "I think there may very well be Legos in heaven. God doesn't tell us for sure. But what I do know is that if there aren't Legos in heaven, there will be toys that are *so* neat and *so* fun, you won't want to play with your Legos anymore." I'm not suggesting that there will be literal toys in heaven. Since we will all be fully matured in heaven, a child's outlook will be changed. (See question #30.)

Children love to receive gifts. Adults do too. Gifts are fun because they usually surprise us with something we like. Explain to children that God is the best gift-giver ever. He gives us many, many good gifts. Heaven is the best of his gifts, and he gives it to the one who simply believes in him. Jesus told a large crowd once, "If you, then, though you are evil, know how to give good gifts to your children, how much more will your Father in heaven give good gifts to those who ask him!" (Matt. 7:11). If a toy is a good gift in heaven for anyone, God will certainly give it!

I might also ask a child, "Who is a person you think is really loving toward you?" I would hope my sons would say that their mom and dad are the ones who love them the most. Some children might think of another relative, their teacher at school, or a friend next door. But I would add, "Jesus loves you a million times more than he or she does. Since he loves you so much, he won't forget to give you all the things you need to have fun in heaven." If we simply define fun as enjoyment and holy pleasure, heaven will definitely be fun. Psalm 16:11 says, "You will fill me . . . with eternal pleasures at your right hand."

Perhaps this sounds strange. Why are we resistant to saying that heaven will be fun? Because we have been misled to think of God as overly strict, unloving, unkind, and un-fun—even though we would never admit such an idea. Fun is defined as enjoyment, entertainment, pleasure. In heaven we will love exactly what we do, and we will do exactly what we love. Everything will be enjoyable and pleasurable. Heaven will be enthralling, captivating, gratifying, thrilling. Do those words sound like it will be fun?

Look at the promises God makes about heaven. "The LORD will withhold no good thing from those who do what is right" (Ps. 84:11 NLT). If Legos will make us happy in heaven, then they will be there! If dolls are essential for us to be satisfied, they will be there. God won't withhold any good gift in heaven.

Jesus told his disciples, "Do not store up for yourselves treasures on earth. . . . But store up for yourselves treasures in heaven" (Matt. 6:19–20). Why did he use the word *treasures* when he spoke of valuable things in heaven? Doesn't that sound contradictory to what we think about heaven? Treasures! He used that word because treasures on earth are things we greatly value. "Treasures in heaven" will be the very things we want the most when we get to heaven.

What's a treasure to a child? Something valuable to them that makes them happy. When a child believes in Jesus as the only one who can forgive his or her sins, he is prepared to love and obey Jesus. By obeying Jesus, a child can store up "Legos" in heaven.

God will change our "want to" in heaven. I didn't learn to enjoy coffee until I was twenty-six. My wife didn't learn to drink coffee until she was over fifty. Now she can't do without that cup of joe in the morning. Our tastes changed. In a similar way, our "tastes" will change in heaven.

FOR FURTHER STUDY

Job 36:11; Psalm 21:6; 36:8; Matthew 25:21, 23; Luke 15:7; John 4:10; 10:10; Romans 8:32

41 If I live in hope of heaven, won't I neglect earthly needs around me?

I've often heard it said, "We can be so heavenly minded that we are of no earthly good." This may be spoken by well-meaning people. Perhaps they have known Christians who were deeply involved in "religious" work but lacked compassion. Yet the Bible does encourage us to think heavenly. C. S. Lewis once said, "Aim at heaven and you will get earth thrown in. Aim at earth and you get neither." No one was more heavenly minded than Jesus, and I don't think Jesus was of no earthly good.

Listen to what Paul said to a church in Asia Minor (present-day Turkey). "Since you have been raised to new life with Christ, set your sights on the realities of heaven, where Christ sits in the place of honor at God's right hand. Think about the things of heaven, not the things of earth" (Col. 3:1–2 NLT). So the Bible tells us plainly to be heavenly minded.

Why? Being heavenly minded, i.e., thinking about and longing for heaven, can help us avoid temptation and sin. The alternative to thinking about heaven is to be thinking about "earthly things." When we think about earthly things, we become susceptible to sinful enticements and wrong values.

By "earthly things," I don't mean our earthly responsibilities and duties. When we are heavenly minded, we will be careful to carry out the obligations we have while on earth. By "earthly things" I mean selfish and temporal values—things that do not carry into eternity and are "idols" that replace God in our hearts. The Holy Spirit told John about a group of faithful believers who would die in the future. He explained that they were greatly blessed because "they will rest from their labor, for their deeds will follow them" (Rev. 14:13). That means their good deeds will be carried into eternity and will be honored and rewarded in heaven by the Lord. How they lived on earth will affect their lives in heaven. God promises to honor his followers who remain faithful. (For more details on this subject, see question #48.)

When Jesus predicted that he must suffer and be put to death by the Jewish leaders in Jerusalem, Peter challenged him never to think such a thing. Jesus replied, "You are a hindrance to me. For you are not setting your mind on the things of God, but on the things of man" (Matt. 16:23 ESV). Peter was rebuked for setting his mind on earthly, human values rather than heavenly values ("the things of God").

C. T. Studd, who gave up a wealthy inheritance to become a missionary to China in the late 1800s, said, "Only one life, it will soon be past; only what is done for Christ will last." Anything that is ever done in human effort and self-reliance will remain on earth. Only those things done for the Lord with pure motives and complete dependence on him will carry on into heaven and eternity.

Being heavenly minded also means that we understand the Lord will one day destroy this earth. Peter challenged, "You ought to live holy and godly lives as you look forward to the day of God. . . . That day will bring about the destruction of the heavens by fire, and the elements will melt in the heat. But in keeping with his promise we are looking forward to a new heaven and a new earth, where righteousness dwells" (2 Peter 3:11–13). The material things of this earth won't last: money, fame, possessions, property, etc. We must invest our lives in what counts.

When we are heavenly minded, we don't have to fear death any longer. We know that death carries us into the comforting presence of Jesus. Many of those who have no certainty of heaven are plagued by fear in the face of death. They desperately cling to life, sometimes searching frantically for measures to prolong life.

Paul looked squarely at death, fully assured of a bodily resurrection. "When the perishable has been clothed with the imperishable, and the mortal with immortality, then the saying that is written [in the Old Testament] will come true: 'Death has been swallowed up in victory.'" Then, as if he were sarcastically laughing right at death, Paul asked, "Where, O death, is your victory? Where, O death, is your sting?" (1 Cor. 15:54–55). That's how confident he was of going to heaven. That's being heavenly minded.

FOR FURTHER STUDY

Psalm 14:1; Jeremiah 17:9; Matthew 6:25–34; 2 Corinthians 4:18; Ephesians 1:3; Philippians 3:20–21; James 3:17

42 What happens to those who are unable to believe in Jesus, like aborted babies, young children, or those who have a severe mental disability?

Few things are more heartbreaking and traumatic than the death of a child. Suppose a Christian family goes to the pool for a swim on a warm summer day. In a heartbeat, while no one is carefully watching, the young daughter drowns. How do we comfort the mother and father of that child? Is their daughter in heaven? Will they ever see their daughter again?

I believe the Bible teaches that the death of Jesus on the cross covers the sins of everyone who believes in him and everyone who is incapable of faith. In other words, Jesus' death is the means by which God can bring the infant, the mentally disabled, or the aborted child into his presence. The Bible teaches that every person is estranged from God and needs a Savior, even children. Children will go to heaven not because they are innocent but because their separation from God is covered by the death of Christ.

After David, king of Israel, committed adultery with Bathsheba and later married her, a child was born out of the illicit relationship. But God told David through Nathan the prophet that the child would die because of David's sin. How did David mourn the death of his child? Did he mourn him as if he would never see the child?

David's attendants were baffled by how he acted. "Why are you acting this way? While the child was alive, you fasted and wept, but now that the child is dead, you get up and eat!" David answered, "While the child was still alive, I fasted and wept. I thought, 'Who knows? The LORD may be gracious to me and let the child live.' But now that he is dead, why should I go on fasting? Can I bring him back again? I will go to him, but he will not return to me" (2 Sam. 12:22–23). This certainly implies that David expected to be in heaven with his child.

Jesus instructed his disciples, "Let the little children come to me, and do not hinder them, for the kingdom of heaven belongs to such as these" (Matt. 19:14). Jesus' attitude toward children in his various teachings seem to indicate that children who die before they are able to believe in him will be in heaven. The Bible doesn't say exactly what age must be reached before a child becomes fully responsible to accept Christ as Savior. This is probably an individual matter for each child.

When the disciples asked Jesus about who would be greatest in his kingdom, Jesus called a little child over to him. "Truly I tell you, unless you change and become like little children, you will never enter the kingdom of heaven. Therefore, whoever takes the lowly position of this child is the greatest in the kingdom of heaven" (Matt. 18:2–4). Jesus was using children as his example of faith. Such a view of children is impossible if Jesus thought of children as being judged and sent to hell for their sins.

Will infants and children still be infants and children in heaven? The Bible doesn't tell us directly. Just as God will erase the evidence of aging in people in the resurrection and for life on the new earth, so it seems most likely God will erase immaturity in the resurrection and for life on the new earth. All those mentally incapable of believing in Jesus will become fully rational in heaven.

Aborted children will also be in heaven. The child in the womb has been a child from conception. He or she is created in God's image and carries a soul. An angel told Zacharias, the father of John the Baptist, that John would be "filled with the Holy Spirit even before he is born" (Luke 1:15). God's Spirit doesn't live in tissue (a fetus) but in people. Later, John the Baptist's mother, Elizabeth, met with Mary, the mother of Jesus. Elizabeth told Mary, "As soon as the sound of your greeting reached my ears, the baby in my womb [John the Baptist] leaped for joy" (v. 44). That "fetus" was called a baby. Babies who are aborted or miscarried have a soul and will also be in heaven.

Christians have very good reasons to encourage other Christians whose children have died that they will be reunited in heaven. However, even though aborted children go to heaven, we should never promote abortion so that an unborn infant goes to heaven. God commands us never to do evil with the intent that good may result.

FOR FURTHER STUDY

Genesis 48:16; Psalm 51:5; 139:13; Matthew 18:10; 19:14; Mark 10:15; Romans 3:8; Galatians 1:15; 1 Peter 2:2

43 What should I do if I am afraid of death?

Corrie ten Boom (1892–1983) lived in the Netherlands in the 1940s when the Nazis invaded the country. She describes in her bestselling book, *The Hiding Place*, how she helped her Christian parents and siblings hide Jews in their home during the Holocaust of World War II. Once, when Corrie was a young girl, a neighbor had died, prompting within her fears for the time when her parents would die. But her father consoled her. "When we go to Amsterdam, when do I give you your train ticket?" Corrie replied, "Just before we get on the train." "So your heavenly Father will give you exactly what you need when we die—and He will give it just when you need it."

Christians sometimes call this "dying grace," i.e., the uncommon strength and confidence that God will give us graciously at the time of our death. If you are a Christian, you can trust our loving Father to give you "your ticket" at the right time—and probably not before you need it. Consider how a baby cries as it comes out of the womb. Why? It is entering a marvelous and beautiful world of sight and sound that it has never experienced before! So why should it be afraid? If it only knew the astounding new world it was entering! So too for the Christian believer, experiencing death and heaven that follows may seem on this side to be frightful. If he or she only knew the astounding beauty and joy of the future age planned for us by our Father!

One of the most comforting and well-known verses of the Bible regarding death is found in Psalm 23. David said to the Lord, "Even though I walk through the valley of the shadow of death, I will fear no evil, for you are with me; your rod and your staff, they comfort me" (v. 4 ESV). Death is a shadowy valley, threatening fearful troubles. But David found great comfort in the Lord. The rod and staff were the implements of a shepherd to guide and protect the sheep. When touched, this gear made the sheep aware of the shepherd's presence. David consistently sensed God's presence in his life to protect and console his heart, even when death seemed imminent.

God is not the source of our fears of death. The fear of death is the power that Satan wields over us until we come to faith in Jesus, who has won the victory over death. "Because God's children are human beings—made of flesh and blood—the Son also became flesh and blood. For only as a human being could he die, and only by dying could he break the power of the devil, who had the power of death. Only in this way could he set free all who have lived their lives as slaves to the fear of dying" (Heb. 2:14–15 NLT). So the only "power over death" that Satan has is to incite the fear of death. Don't let him infuse your thoughts with fear.

For many, death comes after a long life. Old age has a way of helping us long for heaven and overcome the fear of death. When our pains increase and our strength grows weary, heaven becomes more and more desirable, and fear about death loosens.

One wonderful resource we should remember is prayer. God will answer our prayers about the fears of death we have. This is a promise. "Let us then approach God's throne of grace with confidence, so that we may receive mercy and find grace to help us in our time of need" (Heb. 4:16).

Until that time when God calls you home, read and claim the promises of Jesus about eternal life (see "For Further Study" below). Many are quite emphatic and can be found in the gospel of John, the fourth book of the New Testament. John 11:25–26 is a clear example: "Jesus then said, 'I am the one who raises the dead to life! Everyone who has faith in me will live, even if they die. And everyone who lives because of faith in me will never really die'" (CEV).

FOR FURTHER STUDY

Deuteronomy 31:8; Psalm 23; Matthew 10:31; Mark 6:47–51; Luke 12:7; John 20:19; Hebrews 13:6

44 How can I be sure I'm going to heaven?

When I was young, my parents took our family to a small evangelical church each Sunday. The first time I remember placing my faith in Jesus as my Savior was during a Sunday evening service when I was nine or ten. I remember days later, swinging on the swings at the playground of my school, sensing that I was spiritually clean and bound for heaven. But I soon began to doubt whether I was going to heaven. What if I sinned—especially if I sinned willfully? Would I lose the eternal life God had given me? How could I know for sure I was going to heaven?

In my preteen and early teen years, I delivered newspapers on my bike to about a hundred customers every morning except Sunday. Several customers I had were grouchy, complaining types, rarely satisfied with where I tossed their paper. I often asked myself what would happen to me eternally if, in meanness, I purposefully threw their newspaper in an inconvenient spot or left it where the rain would get it all wet. My only conclusion was that my sin would cause me to lose heaven. My childlike solution was to pray, "Lord, please forgive me a minute before each sin I commit." That way I thought I could make it to heaven for sure.

It wasn't until after I graduated from college that I understood the unbreakable, trustworthy nature of Jesus' promise of eternal life. He said, "Very truly I tell you, the one who believes has eternal life" (John 6:47), a guarantee that eternal life is the present possession of anyone who believes in him. Jesus pledged numerous times that "everyone who believes in Him will have eternal life" (John 3:15 HCSB). So if one has believed in Jesus as his or her only hope of eternal life and heaven, that person can claim that he or she has eternal life. Such a claim is not presumption—it is faith. According to the teachings of Jesus, then, it is a contradiction to say you are relying completely on him by faith alone to get you to heaven, but in the next breath you express doubts that you have eternal life.

So in my early twenties, as I saw these truths, I claimed Jesus' promise as my own. I have never doubted my eternal destiny since! I continue to claim Jesus' promise as my only hope of heaven.

Eternal life is a permanent gift from God. I have a Christian friend who says, "If eternal life can be lost, it has the wrong name." How true! Eternal life is forever. Jesus said this in varying but clear ways. "It is my Father's will that whoever sees the Son and believes in him should have eternal life, and that I should raise that person up on the last day" (John 6:40 NJB). According to Jesus, the Father's will was that Jesus resurrect every person who believed in him. Has Jesus ever failed to do the will of his Father? Will he ever fail in the future to do the will of his Father? Do you believe that Jesus is your only means of getting to heaven? Then claim his promise of resurrection and eternal life.

We have all heard someone make a promise that we believed he or she would keep: a political candidate, a bride or bridegroom, a boss, a contractor, etc. We accept human promises even though we know that people often fail to keep them. But God and Jesus never fail to keep their promises. The promises of Jesus are far more trustworthy than any human pledge or vow. Consider again the absolute guarantee of the Lord's promise: "Everyone who lives and believes in Me will never die—ever" (John 11:26 HCSB). Jesus was referring to the impossibility of one who believes in him ever dying an eternal death or experiencing an eternal punishment.

God wants us who believe in Christ to be fully assured of his promise and to know that we have eternal life and heaven.

We accept human testimony, but God's testimony is greater because it is the testimony of God, which he has given about his Son. Whoever believes in the Son of God accepts this testimony. Whoever does not believe God has made him out to be a liar, because they have not believed the testimony God has given about his Son. And this is the testimony: God has given us eternal life, and this life is in his Son. Whoever has the Son has life; whoever does not have the Son of God does not have life. I [the apostle John] write these things to you who believe in the name of the Son of God so that *you may know that you have eternal life.* (1 John 5:9–13, italics added)

God's testimony is that he has given eternal life in Jesus, and that everyone who believes has (right now) eternal life. Ask yourself these simple questions: Do I accept God's testimony? Do I believe in Jesus, God's Son? Then, according to this promise, what do I have? If a person "has the Son," i.e., "believes in the name of the Son of God," what does he or she have? Answer: eternal life. According to this promise, can one who believes in Jesus know that she has eternal life? Of course! Would God lie to us? Certainly not! Then how can we know for sure that we have eternal life and will

121

be in heaven one day? We can know because God promises that it will be so! Read again the italicized words in the quote above.

Some Christians think the Bible teaches that we can only have assurance of heaven if we are living a godly lifestyle. They challenge us to ask ourselves, "Am I living like Christ teaches I should live?" But this can be spiritually defeating. I can always find some inadequacy in my spiritual life that can cause me to doubt my relationship with Christ.

Christlike character reinforces the fact that I am a true Christian. But it is not the basis of my assurance of heaven. Only faith in the Bible's promise of eternal life can give true assurance. Hebrews 11:1 defines faith as our assurance: "Faith is the confidence that what we hope for will actually happen; it gives us assurance about things we cannot see" (NLT). If you are weak in your confidence about being in heaven, then I would suggest reading the gospel of John. See how many times Jesus guarantees eternal life to the one who believes in him for it.

FOR FURTHER STUDY

John 5:24; 6:37–40; 10:27–30; 20:27; Romans 4:18–21; 2 Timothy 1:12

45 What is the great white throne judgment of Revelation 20?

A friend was recently called to jury duty. In the case, a woman had been charged with assault and battery with a deadly weapon. The jury unanimously convicted her. But the final sentencing was to come later. At that time the judge would announce the degree of punishment the woman deserved.

Christians often call the final sentencing of those who reject Jesus as their Savior the "great white throne judgment." The name is derived from a scene in the book of Revelation where the apostle John wrote, "Then I saw a great white throne and him who was seated on it. The earth and the heavens fled from his presence, and there was no place for them" (20:11).

The white throne symbolizes God's purity, holiness, and indisputable justice. John saw that the throne was "great" or large, representing God's unequaled authority. The awesome dignity of the one on the throne caused the earth and the heavens (sun, moon, stars, etc.) to flee from his presence. The sin-stained universe cannot remain in God's holy presence. Because of the initial rebellion of humans in the garden of Eden, God has placed a curse on the earth. It has thwarted human productivity ever since. Science recognizes that things tend to move toward disorder, not order. My desk *never* gets organized by itself.

The one who sits on the throne is Jesus. He himself said, "the Father judges no one, but has entrusted all judgment to the Son" (John 5:22). Jesus, who stepped out of eternity, became a human person, and lived a sinless human life, will be the one who will judge all sinful humans. God's judgment is fair.

Next, John said he "saw the dead, great and small, standing before the throne, and books were opened. Another book was opened, which is the book of life. The dead were judged according to what they had done as recorded in the books" (Rev. 20:12). The books that are opened have a record of everything that everyone has ever done while alive on earth. The point of these books is that all of our deeds, words, thoughts, and emotions will be examined by the Lord.

What is the Book of Life? John explains, "Anyone whose name was not found written in the book of life was thrown into the lake of fire" (20:15). The Book of (eternal) Life contains a list of the names of everyone who has come to faith in Jesus. The lake of fire is the final judgment we usually call hell. The great white throne judgment is a judgment for the one who has rejected Jesus. The books that record their deeds and words, including their hidden motives, will show irrefutably that they are deserving of an eternal judgment.

Some Christians believe that there will be one general judgment for all people. At this single time of judgment, God will determine who has faith in Jesus and has their name written in the Book of Life, and who has not expressed faith in Jesus. But it is more likely that the great white throne judgment is only for unbelievers. Their names are not in the Book of Life and therefore they are judged and condemned based on their deeds.

Believing Christians will escape this judgment because they have eternal life, which includes the forgiveness of all their sins. Their names are written in the Book of Life. Jesus promised, "Whoever believes in [me] is not condemned, but whoever does not believe stands condemned already because they have not believed in the name of God's one and only Son" (John 3:18). Our eternal destiny is ultimately determined on earth.

At the great white throne of judgment, "Hades gave up the dead that were in them, and each person was judged according to what they had done. Then death and Hades were thrown into the lake of fire" (Rev. 20:13–14). Hades is the temporary place of confinement for all those who have rejected Jesus. (For more detail about Hades, see question #34.) They are judged "according to what they had done" (v. 12). Since they are already in Hades, their eternal destiny is both known and fixed. The great white throne judgment determines that they really deserve to be in the lake of fire, and it determines what degree of punishment they should have.

There are degrees of punishment in hell. Jesus criticized the people in a town called Capernaum for not responding in faith to his miracles. "I tell you," he said, "that it will be more bearable for Sodom on the day of judgment than for you" (Matt. 11:24). The Old Testament city of Sodom was so wicked that God destroyed it completely. The words "it will be more bearable" suggest that the evil people of Sodom will have a lesser punishment in the lake of fire [= hell] than the people of Capernaum. Greater exposure to truth brings greater responsibility.

FOR FURTHER STUDY

Daniel 7:9–14; Matthew 10:14–15; 12:36; 25:31–46; Acts 17:30–31; 24:25; Romans 2:5; Jude 6

46 What does the Bible call the "judgment seat of Christ"?

Most jobs have some kind of performance review. The employee receives an evaluation of his or her performance, with comments on successes and failures, on weaknesses and strengths, etc. Sometimes a promotion or demotion is the result, and salaries are increased or decreased. One could even be fired from the job at a performance review. So performance reviews can be a little threatening.

Paul wrote all of his thirteen New Testament letters to various Christian churches and church leaders. But they were intended to be read and applied by all Christians. To the Christians at Corinth, he wrote, "We make it our goal to please him [the Lord] . . . For we [Christians] must all appear before the judgment seat of Christ, so that each of us may receive what is due us for the things done while in the body, whether good or bad" (2 Cor. 5:9–10). By the term *judgment seat of Christ*, Paul was referring to the ultimate performance review that each believing Christian will have one day.

The judgment seat of Christ will not determine a person's eternal destiny. As mentioned before, that determination is made while we are on earth. At death, the Christian goes immediately into the presence of Christ. There is no need to explain to her where she will spend eternity! It will be more than obvious since she is in great happiness in the presence of Jesus. At the judgment seat of Christ, he will examine the faithfulness of each believer. Was his life worthy to receive a commendation from the Lord? Should she be rewarded for the sacrifices she made for Jesus?

The word for "judgment seat" was a common word in Greek and Roman culture. Pilate sat on a judgment seat when he appeared in public to decide whether or not to crucify Jesus (John 19:13). A judgment seat was also an elevated platform on which judge(s) sat during the ancient Olympic games. From this platform, the judge could disqualify a contestant or award a victory crown to the winning athlete.

How will this evaluation of the true Christian take place? Paul used the analogy of a building to represent a Christian's life. The foundation of the building is Jesus. Christians are the builders. Paul warned, "Each one should build with care" (1 Cor. 3:10). Will he build carefully onto his foundation, his initial faith in Jesus as Savior?

> If anyone builds on this foundation using gold, silver, costly stones, wood, hay or straw, their work will be shown for what it is, because the Day will bring it to light. It will be revealed with fire, and the fire will test the quality of each person's work. If what has been built survives, the builder will receive a reward. If it is burned up, the builder will suffer loss but yet will be saved—even though only as one escaping through the flames. (1 Cor. 3:12–15)

Everything we have done as true Christians will be tested one day. The fire Paul mentions here is not hell. It is symbolic just like the materials (gold, silver, etc.) are symbolic. Things we have done faithfully for the Lord with pure motives will be like precious metals. Metals going through a fire are purified and remain unharmed. Gold, silver, and costly stones are our commendable actions and good works. But Christians who have lived in ways

126

that do not honor Jesus will have actions and words (wood, hay, straw) that "are burned up" and so do not remain for eternity and are not rewarded.

The disobedient believer might "suffer loss." But this is not the loss of his or her salvation. That person "will be saved." It is like a man who flees too late from a burning home to rescue many of his possessions. Even attitudes such as a persistent judgmental spirit can cause us to lose a reward. Paul warned, "You, then, why do you judge your [Christian] brother or sister? Or why do you treat them with contempt? For we will all stand before God's judgment seat" (Rom. 14:10).

Jesus said the same: "Do not judge, or you too will be judged. For in the same way you judge others, you will be judged, and with the measure you use, it will be measured to you" (Matt. 7:1–2). If we are unmerciful to others, Jesus will use the very same standard in our future evaluation. At that time each of us will desperately want and need his mercy and grace instead.

This future performance review before the Lord will be an individual assessment. We will not be judged corporately with some other group like the church we attended or an organization we gave money to. No true Christian will be excused from this judgment, even apostles like Peter and Paul. What will be weighed is the quality of a person's life and works, not the quantity of things he or she has done.

FOR FURTHER STUDY

Proverbs 11:18; Isaiah 40:10; 62:11; Matthew 6:16–21; Luke 12:47–48; Hebrews 11:25–26; 2 John 8; Revelation 2:23

47 Will others in heaven know my secret sins on earth?

All of us who have come to faith in Jesus have had sinful thoughts, spoken sinful words, and done sinful things for which we've been ashamed. Paul wrote to the Roman Christians, "What benefit did you reap at that time [before faith in Jesus] from the things you are now ashamed of?" (Rom. 6:21). None of us wants to have all our sins exposed for others to see or hear—either now or in heaven. We would hope that God would not expose all these secret sins in his final evaluation of us.

God has exposed many of the secret sins of people on earth. King David's secret adultery was openly recorded in the Bible for countless millions of people to read. Yet God said of David that he was "a man after my own heart; he will do everything I want him to do" (Acts 13:22). David is called a man after God's heart because, among many reasons, David confessed his sin to God and repented.

Everyone who reads the New Testament knows that Peter denied Jesus three times and afterward wept bitterly (Matt. 26:75). As the early church began to increase, a Christian couple named Ananias and Sapphira sold a piece of property. They gave some of the price of the sale to the apostles for the needs of the believers among them. But they lied. They gave the impression that they had given as a gift the entire price of the sale. God exposed their hypocrisy to all and then they both died sudden deaths (Acts 5:1–11). I suspect we will recall the lives of David, Peter, Ananias, and Sapphira in heaven along with their sins. These secret sins were made known publicly. If some of their secret sins were openly exposed, why should we think that God will keep our secret sins a secret?

Some verses appear to say this very thing. Jesus said, "There is nothing concealed that will not be disclosed, or hidden that will not be made known" (Matt. 10:26). Elsewhere the New Testament says, "Nothing in all creation is hidden from God's sight. Everything is uncovered and laid bare before the eyes of him to whom we must give account" (Heb. 4:13). Paul also said that when the Lord returns, "He will bring to light what is hidden in darkness and will expose the motives of the heart" (1 Cor. 4:5). Some of these verses could refer only to the unbelieving person. But in this last verse, Paul had believing Christians specifically in mind (see vv. 1–2).

If the Lord reveals everything about our lives to all others in heaven, no one will ever be able to say, "How come Sam was so greatly praised and rewarded by Jesus, but Sally wasn't? That seems unfair!" If all things are revealed, then we will all see the astounding equity (and grace) of God in praising the life of one believer, and showing disapproval for the life of another. We will all agree: "God does not show favoritism" (Rom. 2:11).

But let me offer this important limitation. The verses I've mentioned about exposing hidden sins were written to encourage all Christian readers to deal with secret sins by confessing them to the Lord and repenting. The Lord does not need to openly display in heaven a secret sin that has been confessed and overcome in the power of the Lord. There would be little benefit from this. But the person who outwardly appears to be godly, altruistic, or loving but is secretly living a sinful life will find his or her hypocrisy uncovered in heaven.

Jesus often warned against the outward display of kindness and devotion to God. "Take heed that you do not do your charitable deeds before men, to be seen by them. Otherwise you have no reward from your Father in heaven. . . . But when you do a charitable deed, do not let your left hand know what your right hand is doing, that your charitable deed may be in secret; and your Father who sees in secret will Himself reward you openly" (Matt. 6:1, 3–4 NKJV).

Make sure that what is revealed in heaven to everyone else is not your secret sins but your secret benevolence.

FOR FURTHER STUDY

1 Chronicles 28:9; Psalm 32:1–5; 90:8; 139:1–4; Ecclesiastes 12:14; Jeremiah 16:17; Luke 12:2–3; 1 Peter 3:3–4

48 What are "heavenly crowns"?

Sports are big in the media. One statistic suggests that sports comprise 27 percent of weekend TV airtime. Most newscasts include the latest in scores and highlights. If you have cable, you can find a sports event at almost any hour of the day or night.

I can't say that the apostle Paul ever played sports. But he was familiar with sports competitions of his day. He compared the Christian life both to running a race and engaging in a boxing match. To the Christians in the city of Corinth, Paul wrote,

> Do you not know that in a race all the runners run, but only one gets the prize? Run in such a way as to get the prize. Everyone who competes in the games goes into strict training. They do it to get a crown that will not last, but we do it to get a crown that will last forever. Therefore I do not run like someone running aimlessly . . . so that after I have preached to others, I myself will not be disqualified for the prize. (1 Cor. 9:24–27)

Paul was thinking of the famous Isthmian games held near Corinth. These games were a biennial athletic competition second only to the Olympian games of Greece, founded in 776 BC. Victors in these Greek games received a crown made of withered celery plants. Christians who are found to be faithful at the judgment seat of Christ (see question #46) will be rewarded with crowns that will never wither or perish. They are like a victorious runner who is the first to cross the finish line. But like with any athletic competition, serious training and self-discipline are involved. Paul disciplined himself spiritually so that he would not be disqualified for the heavenly prize.

Various crowns given to believers are mentioned in the Bible. These crowns are symbolic of the commendation and reward the trustworthy followers of Christ will receive. One crown is the "crown of life," given to those who faithfully endure persecution or suffering because of their love for Jesus: "Blessed is the one who perseveres under trial because, having stood the test, that person will receive the crown of life that the Lord has promised to those who love him" (James 1:12). Revelation 2:10 also mentions this blessing: "Don't be afraid of what you are about to suffer. . . . Be faithful until death, and I will give you the crown of life" (HCSB). The "crown of life" is a blessing added to the eternal life the true Christian will experience in heaven.

As Paul was near the time he would be martyred, he wrote to his young apprentice, Timothy, "The time for my departure is near. I have fought the good fight, I have finished the race, I have kept the faith. Now there is in store for me the crown of righteousness, which the Lord, the righteous Judge, will award to me on that day—and not only to me, but also to all who have longed for his appearing" (2 Tim. 4:6–8). Since Paul knew he had finished well, he anticipated receiving a crown or reward for his godly and righteous life.

Lance Armstrong, the American cyclist, won seven consecutive Tour de France races between 1999 and 2005. But in 2012 he was disqualified, stripped of his titles, and barred from racing because of illegal drug use during competition.

Even after a follower of Christ has lived obediently for many years, he could become seriously disobedient and be disqualified for reward. Jesus counseled the Philadelphian church, one of the seven churches addressed in Revelation, "Hold on to what you have, so that no one will take your crown" (3:11). To "take away a crown"

131

was a metaphor for being disqualified in an athletic contest. Eternal life cannot be taken away, but future rewards can be.

A heavenly scene in Revelation describes twenty-four elders (faithful Christians) throwing their crowns before the throne of God.

> [They] fall down before him who sits on the throne and worship him who lives for ever and ever. They lay their crowns before the throne and say: "You are worthy, our Lord and God, to receive glory and honor and power." (4:9–11)

By casting their crowns before the throne of God, these faithful Christians were acknowledging that their crowns (rewards) were the result of God's grace and strength. Those who receive these crowns will always be giving credit in eternity to God for his grace in helping them live faithfully.

FOR FURTHER STUDY

Galatians 2:2; 5:7; Philippians 3:14; 4:1; 1 Thessalonians 2:19; 1 Timothy 1:18; 2 Timothy 2:4–5; 1 Peter 5:2–4

49 Why will some believers rule with Christ over the new earth?

When an individual runs for the office of president of the United States, the candidate gathers around him those who will work hard for him as he campaigns. He chooses a campaign committee to advise him and serve his candidacy. If he wins the election, those committee members who stuck with him through the uncertain and difficult times of the candidacy will be rewarded. Often they will become the members of his inner council, the presidential cabinet. Some of them will serve side by side with the newly elected president the entire time he is in the White House.

One day Jesus will return to become president (or king) of the entire world. He will set up a kingdom or empire on the earth. Jesus taught his disciples to pray for that future kingdom in what many Christians call the Lord's Prayer. "Our Father in heaven, hallowed be your name, [may] your kingdom come, [may] your will be done, on earth as it is in heaven" (Matt. 6:9–10). In Jesus' future kingdom, God's desires—his moral standards and righteousness—will be done on the new earth.

When Jesus sets up his kingdom on the new earth, he will have a "President's Cabinet," a large group of those who will rule and counsel with him. Some may rule over larger groups like governors, senators, and representatives. Others may rule over smaller groups like mayors, council members, and city council members. These key leaders will be the faithful ones who have rejected the sinful pleasures of the world and have endured persecution from those who hate and reject Jesus. Jesus made this promise: "To the one who is victorious and does my will to the end [of life], I will give authority over the nations—that one 'will rule them with an iron scepter' . . . just as I have received authority from my Father'" (Rev. 2:26–27).

The Nike shoe company takes its name from Nike, the winged Greek goddess of victory. The word for "victorious" in the original Greek manuscripts is *nikaō,* closely related to the name of that Greek goddess. Those who are victorious in Christian living will be in Jesus' "cabinet" in eternity. Jesus gave the same promise to his followers in another church addressed in Revelation. "To the one who is victorious, I will give the right to sit with me on my throne, just as I was victorious and sat down with my Father on his throne" (3:21).

In one of Jesus' parables, he described a "man of noble birth" (alluding to himself) who had gone to a distant land and was appointed

133

as king. This man's journey describes Jesus' ascension to heaven after his death and resurrection. Before he had left, he gave each of three servants three months' wages to invest. Later, when the king came back and began his reign, he called his servants to account. The first servant multiplied his master's money ten times over, so the master highly commended him and appointed him ruler over ten of the cities in his empire.

The second also invested his master's money, multiplying it five times. The king appointed him over five cities.

The last servant hid the money away, too fearful to invest it. When he returned the money to the king, he was severely rebuked and received no cities to rule over (see Luke 19:11–27).

Jesus was teaching crucial life lessons. First, although the gifts and opportunities he gives us may differ, the Christian believer must invest them all (use them) for the cause of the king (Jesus). Those who do will be given trusted leadership positions in the new earth. Second, different levels of faithfulness will be rewarded accordingly.

In the apostle Paul's very last biblical letter, he wrote from jail to his young disciple named Timothy: "Here is a trustworthy saying: . . . If we endure, we will also reign with him" (2 Tim. 2:11–12). To "reign with him" means to rule along with Jesus in his future kingdom on the new earth. The era in which the American culture respected the believing Christian is past. Many now openly ridicule the faithful follower of Jesus. The believer must persevere in these sufferings by holding to the truth of the Bible.

In its very first chapter, God announced that he would create humans so that they would rule over the earth. "Let us make mankind in our image," he said, "in our likeness, so that they may rule [over the earth] . . ." (Gen. 1:26). But sin enticed and entered humanity, and this rulership over the world was drastically restricted. Through the sacrifice of Jesus on the cross, God restored his relationship with people who believe in Jesus and has been preparing them to rule on the earth once again. In the last chapter of the Bible, we read, "His servants will serve him. . . . And they will reign for ever and ever" (Rev. 22:3–5).

FOR FURTHER STUDY

Jeremiah 33:15; Daniel 7:27; Zechariah 9:10; Matthew 6:16–21; Luke 19:11–27; 2 Peter 3:13; Revelation 5:10; 19:11–16

50 What can I do to prepare for eternity in heaven?

Any time we take a trip, there is by necessity a lot of planning and preparation. First and foremost will be the destination. We will need to know exactly where we want to go. I recently took a trip to see family in Pennsylvania. I put into my cell phone's GPS the name of the small town where I wanted to go, but no address. I thought the GPS would lead me to the very center of the town; I could remember the location of my brother's home from there. Instead, the GPS led me to a dead end of a subdivision at the end of town. I got lost.

We need to make sure we have the right directions for going to heaven. Without the right directions, we are lost forever. If you are going to a U.S. town called Greenville, you had better get the right directions! Every state in the Union but one has a town called Greenville. Who knows where you'll end up. (For more about the way to heaven, see questions #1, #2, and #44.)

After we are sure of our destination, we will want to identify what we need to take with us for the trip. I get a little nervous about upcoming trips since I don't want to leave anything behind that I might need at my destination. Did I get all the shirts I'll need? I don't want to wear the same shirt for three days.

It's also essential that we start planning now for our trip to heaven. Some things we can't take with us. Other things we can send on ahead of us. In 1989, Aurora Schuck of (coincidently) Aurora, Indiana, was buried in her beloved 1976 Cadillac convertible. Her husband had the oil changed and the gas tank filled before the burial. In 2002, when he died, he was buried next to his wife. The car had not moved. Wherever the couple went after death, they didn't drive there.

You probably know that you can't take any possessions or accumulated wealth with you to heaven. But you can invest your money on earth in such a way that you will have riches in heaven. Jesus talked more about money than about any other subject. Jesus once said, "Do not store up for yourselves treasures on earth, where moths and vermin destroy, and where thieves break in and steal. But store up for yourselves treasures in heaven, where moths and vermin do not destroy, and where thieves do not break in and steal" (Matt. 6:19–20).

"Money is the root of all evil." That saying is perhaps the most misquoted verse of the Bible. The verse actually reads, "The *love of* money is a root of all kinds of evil" (1 Tim. 6:10). That's quite different. Jesus wasn't against savings accounts or investing in the stock market. He was suggesting that all these earthly investments are temporary compared to "investing" our money in the "bank" of heaven. His point was this: "Where your treasure is, there your heart will be also" (Matt. 6:21). Those who invest heavily in the stock market often keep up on the stock market news every day. Their heart could become focused on their investments. But if we send our money on ahead of us to heaven, our daily focus will become heavenly oriented.

I once read of a wealthy businessman who collected numerous classic and antique cars. Tragically, he crashed while driving his own car and died. At the time of his death, his collection amounted to more than 880 cars. To liquidate his estate, the collection was sold at car auctions over the next several years.

Jesus told a parable of a man who had an abundant harvest of grain and planned to build bigger buildings to hold it all. But before the rich man even started building, God spoke to him. "You fool! This very night your life will be demanded from you. Then who will get what you have prepared for yourself?" Jesus concluded, "This is how it will be with whoever stores up things for themselves but is not rich toward God" (Luke 12:20–21).

How can we become rich toward God? One way is to give generously to the poor. Jesus taught us that "it is more blessed to give than to receive" (see Acts 20:35). But the first priority of this giving is to be for other poor believers, not only poor people in general. Paul wrote, "As we have opportunity, let us do good to all people, especially to those who belong to the family of believers" (Gal. 6:10).

We are also to give our money for ministries that spread the message of Jesus. Paul wrote a thank-you note to the Philippians for joining with him financially in spreading the message about forgiveness through Jesus. "You Philippians know from the time of my first mission work in Macedonia how no church shared in supporting my ministry except you. You sent contributions repeatedly" (Phil. 4:15–16 CEB).

When Jesus was asked if it was right to pay taxes to the emperor Caesar, he asked for a coin. "Whose image is on this coin?" he asked. They replied, "Caesar's." Then Jesus challenged them, "So give back to Caesar what is Caesar's, and to God what is God's" (Matt. 22:15–21). The coin with Caesar's image could pay the Romans their taxes. But what has God's image stamped on it? We do! We have been made in God's image (Gen. 1:26–27). So Jesus was implying that we must give back to him *ourselves*. We must yield ourselves to God in complete submission. We must become his disciples. That's the least we can do for all he has done for us!

FOR FURTHER STUDY

Jeremiah 22:16; Matthew 6:22–24; Luke 21:1–4; Acts 2:43–45; 2 Corinthians 9:5–13; 1 Timothy 6:17–19

John Hart is Professor of Bible at the Moody Bible Institute. He received his ThM from Dallas Theological Seminary and his ThD from Grace Theological Seminary.

More Answers Straight From God's Word

Find comfort and peace in the truth about heaven, straight from the Bible. In this brief volume, every scriptural reference to heaven has been carefully collected and commentated on.

Everything the Bible Says About Heaven

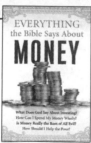

Supernatural beings fascinate us because they are so mysterious. By exploring Scripture passages that mention angels and demons, this book will help quench your curiosity and rest your fears.

Everything the Bible Says About Angels and Demons

How people deal with money matters to God. In this concise volume, hear what God has to say about everything related to the subject, including working, saving, tithing—and more!

Everything the Bible Says About Money

◊ BETHANYHOUSE

Stay up-to-date on your favorite books and authors with our free e-newsletters. Sign up today at bethanyhouse.com.

Find us on Facebook. facebook.com/BHPnonfiction

Follow us on Twitter. @bethany_house